elizabeth hartman

modern PATCH work

12 Quilts to Take You Beyond the Basics

stash BOOKS.

an imprint of C&T Publishing

Text copyright © 2012 by Elizabeth Hartman

Photography and Artwork copyright © 2012 by C&T Publishing, Inc.

PUBLISHER | Amy Marson

CREATIVE DIRECTOR | Gailen Runge

EDITORS | Lynn Koolish and Phyllis Elving

TECHNICAL EDITORS | Nanette Zeller and Alison Schmidt

COVER/BOOK DESIGNER | Kristy Zacharias

PRODUCTION COORDINATOR | Jenny Davis

PRODUCTION EDITOR | Alice Mace Nakanishi

ILLUSTRATOR | Wendy Mathson

PHOTOGRAPHY BY Christina Carty-Francis and Diane Pedersen of C&T Publishing, Inc., unless otherwise noted

Published by Stash Books, an imprint of C&T Publishing, Inc., P.O. Box 1456, Lafayette, CA 94549

Library of Congress Cataloging-in-Publication Data

Hartman, Elizabeth (Elizabeth Anne)

Modern patchwork : 12 quilts to take you beyond the basics / Elizabeth Hartman.

p. cm.

ISBN 978-1-60705-548-8 (soft cover)

1. Patchwork quilts. 2. Quilting--Patterns. I. Title.

TT835.H342185 2012

746.46'041--dc23

2011040928

Printed in China

10 9 8 7 6 5 4 3 2 1

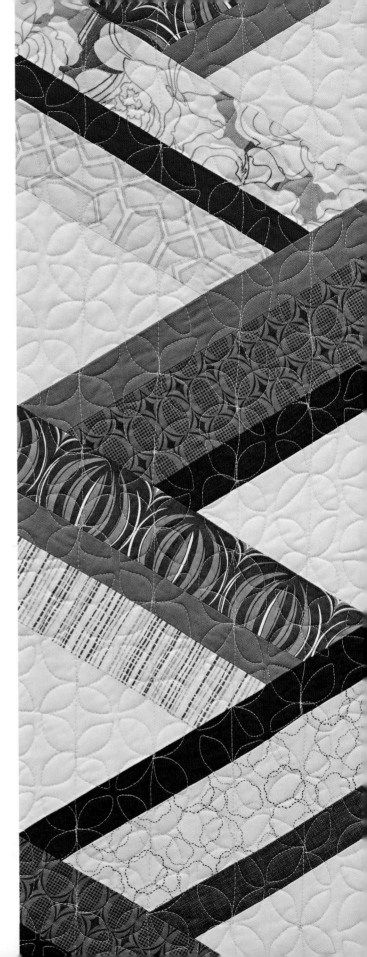

Contents

Dedication

This book is dedicated to all the modern quilters out there who are doing their own thing and creating something beautiful.

Acknowledgments

Thank you to my husband, Chris Hartman, for his support of this project, and to my Portland sewing circle for making the past year so much fun.

Thank you to everyone at C&T Publishing for all your hard work in making this book a reality.

Thank you also to Robert Kaufman Fabrics, Cloud9 Fabrics, Daisy Janie, and Art Gallery Fabrics for generously providing me with fabric to use for this book, and a huge thank-you to Jill Collins for her help with drafting the template patterns.

Introduction

I consider myself a modern quilter, which is sometimes hard to define. In the simplest terms, I think it means that I embrace a clean, modern aesthetic and that I'm more concerned about what works for me than about following a previously established set of rules.

These days it's not hard to find patterns for modern quilting. Many of these are promoted as being quick and simple, which has drawn criticism from some traditionalists. While I disagree that modern quilting is by nature simplistic and unstructured, there does seem to be a dearth of more challenging patterns for modern quilters. Some suggest that modern quilters should just make traditional blocks instead. That's a fine idea in theory, but what if we don't care for the look of traditional blocks? What if we want to make something stylish that we can use in our homes now?

I firmly believe that expanding your skills and taking on new challenges doesn't necessarily mean making traditional blocks. My goal with this book has been to create a set of modern patterns for intermediate-level quilters that promote precision piecing and thoughtful fabric selection, introduce new challenges, and—most important—produce beautiful, stylish quilts that will fit into your modern home.

If you're fairly new to quilting, some of the projects in this book may involve techniques that you haven't tried before or more precise piecing than you're used to. Don't let that scare you off! Making a quilt takes time and, often, trial and error. Creating a beautiful quilt that you can use for years to come is worth the effort!

If you are a beginner or need a refresher course on quiltmaking basics, refer to Materials, Supplies, and More (page 120) and Construction Basics (page 127). For more information, my book The Practical Guide *to Patchwork* provides everything else you might need to know.

Projects

Metropolis

Finished block: 15″ × 15″   **Finished quilt:** 75″ × 75″   *Made and machine quilted by Elizabeth Hartman*

Blocks are sewn and sliced and sewn and sliced again for this quilt top, resulting in a striking woven look that is intricate without being fussy. Setting the blocks in a sea of neutral fabric gives the impression of artwork hanging in a gallery, while the quilt back features an eye-popping giant version of the single block.

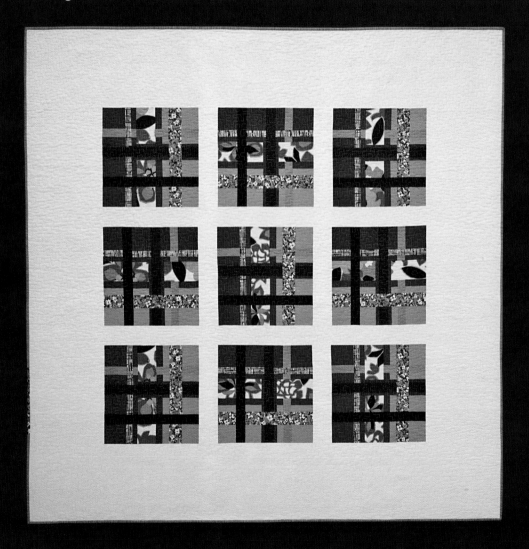

Selecting the Fabric

I started with three multicolor prints that include cream, sea green, gold, gray, and chocolate brown. Then I filled out my selection with six coordinating monochromatic print and solid fabrics that highlight the multicolor prints without overpowering them or making the composition too busy.

Refer to Fabric and Design Vocabulary (page 120) for more about fabric selection.

> **tip** When choosing a solid fabric to coordinate with a print, focus more on highlighting the colors in the print than on trying to match them exactly. Sometimes a solid fabric that is slightly different is more visually interesting.

My fabric choices for Metropolis

materials

Yardages are based on fabric that is at least 40˝ wide, unless otherwise noted.

2¼ yards dark sea green solid fabric (Fabric 1)

2⅛ yards light sea green solid fabric (Fabric 2)

¾ yard gold solid fabric (Fabric 3)

1⅓ yards multicolor print fabric #1 (Fabric 4)

⅞ yard medium brown print fabric (Fabric 5)

⅝ yard multicolor print fabric #2, at least 42˝ wide (Fabric 6)

1⅝ yards chocolate brown print fabric (Fabric 7)

1¾ yards multicolor print fabric #3 (Fabric 8)

2½ yards chocolate brown solid fabric (Fabric 9)

3⅝ yards neutral solid sashing fabric

⅝ yard binding fabric

79˝ × 79˝ batting

Stick-on labels

cutting instructions

 tip Take a moment and use the stick-on labels to label each fabric with its number (1 through 9), as listed in the materials list. As you cut, transfer the labels to the corresponding stacks of block units. Label the 41 pieces for the quilt back as you cut them, using the unique code indicated in the cutting instructions (1A, 2B, and so on).

FABRIC 1 (DARK SEA GREEN SOLID):

Cut:

- 2 strips 22″ × width of fabric; subcut into:

    1 piece 22″ × 22″ (1A)

    1 piece 18¼″ × 22″ (1D)

    1 piece 13″ × 22″ (1C)

    2 pieces 5½″ × 22″ (1B and 1I)

    1 piece 4¼″ × 22″ (1E)

- 1 strip 4¼″ × width of fabric; subcut into:

    1 piece 18¼″ × 4¼″ (1H)

    1 piece 13″ × 4¼″ (1G)

    1 piece 5½″ × 4¼″ (1F)

- 1 strip 5½″ × width of fabric; subcut into:

    1 piece 18¼″ × 5½″ (1L)

    1 piece 13″ × 5½″ (1K)

    1 piece 5½″ × 5½″ (1J)

    Set all the above pieces aside for the quilt back.

- 2 strips 11¾″ × width of fabric; subcut into 9 pieces 6¾″ × 11¾″ (Block Unit 1), and set these aside for the quilt blocks

FABRIC 2 (LIGHT SEA GREEN SOLID):

Cut:

- 2 strips 18¼″ × width of fabric; subcut into:

    1 piece 18¼″ × 18¼″ (2H)

    1 piece 13″ × 18¼″ (2G)

    1 piece 5½″ × 18¼″ (2F)

    1 piece 22″ × 18¼″ (2E)

- 2 strips 5½″ × width of fabric; subcut into:

    1 piece 18¼″ × 5½″ (2D)

    1 piece 13″ × 5½″ (2C)

    1 piece 5½″ × 5½″ (2B)

    1 piece 22″ × 5½″ (2A)

    Set all the above pieces aside for the quilt back.

- 2 strips 11¾″ × width of fabric; subcut into 9 pieces 4¾″ × 11¾″ (Block Unit 2) and set these aside for the quilt blocks

FABRIC 3 (GOLD SOLID):

Cut:

- 2 strips 6¾″ × width of fabric; subcut into:

    1 piece 18¼″ × 6¾″ (3D)

    1 piece 10½″ × 6¾″ (3C)

    1 piece 4¼″ × 6¾″ (3B)

    1 piece 22″ × 6¾″ (3A)

    Set these aside for the quilt back.

- 3 strips 1¾″ × width of fabric; subcut into 9 pieces 11″ × 1¾″ (Block Unit 3) and set these aside for the quilt blocks

CONTINUED ON PAGE 10

FABRIC 4 (MULTICOLOR PRINT #1):

Cut:

- 2 strips 15½″ × width of fabric; subcut into:

  1 piece 33¼″ × 15½″ (4A)

  1 piece 18¼″ × 15½″ (4C)

  1 piece 13″ × 15½″ (4B)

  Set these aside for the quilt back.

- 1 strip 12½″ × width of fabric; subcut into 9 pieces 3½″ × 12½″ (Block Unit 4) and set these aside for the quilt blocks

FABRIC 5 (MEDIUM BROWN PRINT):

Cut:

- 5 strips 3″ × width of fabric; subcut into:

  2 pieces 29¼″ × 3″ (5C and 5D)

  2 pieces 22″ × 3″ (5A and 5B)

  2 pieces 18¼″ × 3″ (5E and 5F)

  Set these aside for the quilt back.

- 1 strip 13½″ × width of fabric; subcut into 9 pieces 2″ × 13½″ (Block Unit 5) and set these aside for the quilt blocks

FABRIC 6 (MULTICOLOR PRINT #2):

Cut:

- 2 strips 5½″ × width of fabric; subcut into:

  1 piece 35¾″ × 5½″ (6A)

  1 piece 18¼″ × 5½″ (6C)

  1 piece 15½″ × 5½″ (6B)

  Set these aside for the quilt back.

- 3 strips 1½″ × width of fabric; subcut into 9 pieces 13½″ × 1½″ (Block Unit 6) and set these aside for the quilt blocks

note | Up to this point, everything has been cut along the width of the fabric. The next few fabrics need to be cut along the length of the fabric (page 128).

FABRIC 7 (CHOCOLATE BROWN PRINT):

Trim away the selvage and cut:

- 2 strips 8″ × length of fabric; subcut into:

  1 piece 55¾″ × 8″ (7A)

  1 piece 18¼″ × 8″ (7B)

  Set these aside for the quilt back.

From the remaining fabric, cut:

- 9 pieces 2″ × 14″ (Block Unit 7) and set these aside for the quilt blocks

FABRIC 8 (MULTICOLOR PRINT #3):

Trim away the selvage and cut:

- 2 strips 10½″ × length of fabric; subcut into:

  1 piece 58¼″ × 10½″ (8A)

  1 piece 18¼″ × 10½″ (8B)

  Set these aside for the quilt back.

From the remaining fabric, cut:

- 9 pieces 2½″ × 14½″ (Block Unit 8) and set these aside for the quilt blocks

FABRIC 9 (CHOCOLATE BROWN SOLID):

Trim away the selvage and cut:

- 1 strip 8″ × length of fabric; trim to 83½″ × 8″ (9A) and set aside for the quilt back

From the remaining fabric, cut:

- 9 pieces 2″ × 15½″ (Block Unit 9) and set aside for the quilt blocks

NEUTRAL SOLID SASHING FABRIC:

Trim away the selvage and cut:

- 2 strips 12½″ × length of fabric; subcut into:

  2 long border strips 75½″ × 12½″

  2 short border strips 51½″ × 12½″

- 2 strips 3½″ × length of fabric; subcut into:

  2 long sashing strips 51½″ × 3½″

  6 short sashing strips 15½″ × 3½″

BINDING FABRIC:

- Cut 8 strips 2½″ × width of fabric.

Making the Blocks

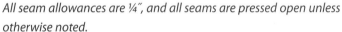

All seam allowances are ¼˝, and all seams are pressed open unless otherwise noted.

1. Sew Block Unit 1 to Block Unit 2, matching the 11¾˝ sides. (Figure A)

2. Measure 3¾˝ down from the top and cut the block horizontally, keeping the cut parallel to the top of the block and at right angles to the seam you've just sewn. Sew the 2 pieces back together with a Block Unit 3 piece between them. (Figure B)

3. Measure 1¼˝ over from the seam joining Block Unit 1 to Block Unit 2 and cut the block vertically, keeping the cut square with the seams you've already sewn. Sew the 2 pieces back together with a Block Unit 4 piece between them. (Figure C)

note

> For the remaining block steps, take care to keep all the cuts square with the seams you've already sewn. Refer to the illustrations as a guide for your cutting.

4. Measure 1½˝ down from the bottom of Block Unit 3 and cut the block horizontally. Sew the 2 pieces back together with a Block Unit 5 piece between them. (Figure D)

5. Measure 1˝ over from the left side of Block Unit 4 and cut the block vertically. Sew the 2 pieces back together with a Block Unit 6 piece between them. (Figure E)

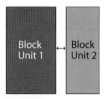

Block Unit 1 ↔ Block Unit 2

Figure A

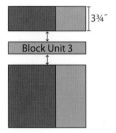

3¾˝

Block Unit 3

Figure B

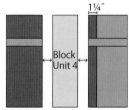

1¼˝

Block Unit 4

Figure C

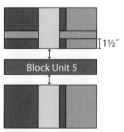

1½˝

Block Unit 5

Figure D

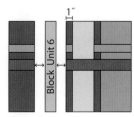

1˝

Block Unit 6

Figure E

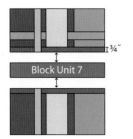

Figure F

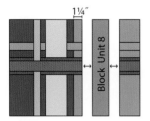

Figure G

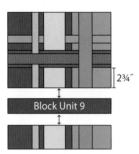

Figure H

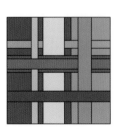

Finished Metropolis *block*

6. Measure ¾˝ down from the top of Block Unit 5 and cut the block in half horizontally, right through the center of Block Unit 5. Sew the 2 pieces back together with a Block Unit 7 piece between them. (Figure F)

7. Measure 1¼˝ over from the seam between Block Unit 1 and Block Unit 2 and cut the block vertically. Sew the 2 pieces back together with a Block Unit 8 piece between them. (Figure G)

8. Measure 2¾˝ down from the bottom of Block Unit 5 and cut the block horizontally. Sew the 2 pieces back together with a Block Unit 9 piece between them. (Figure H)

9. Square up the finished block to 15½˝ × 15½˝.

Repeat Steps 1–9 to make a total of 9 blocks.

Making the Quilt Top

1. Arrange 3 rows of 3 blocks each, rotating every other block 90°. Sew each row together, inserting short sashing strips between adjacent blocks as shown in the quilt top assembly diagram (below). Sew the rows together, inserting long sashing strips between rows.

2. Sew a short border strip to each side and a long border strips to the top and the bottom.

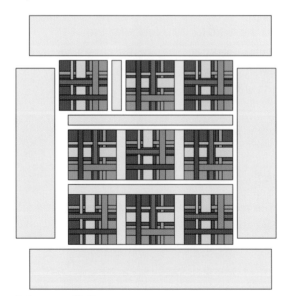

Quilt top assembly diagram

Making the Quilt Back

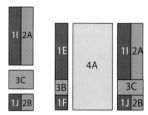

Figure A   **Figure B**

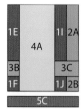

Figure C

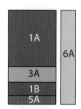

Figure D

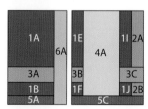

Figure E

Figure F

Figure G

1. Sew 1I to 2A, matching the long sides. Sew 1J to 2B. Sew the 2 pieced units together with 3C between them. Set aside. (Figure A)

2. Sew 1E, 3B, and 1F together, matching the short sides. Sew this unit to the left long side of 4A. Sew the pieced unit from Step 1 to the right side of 4A. (Figure B)

3. Sew 5C to the bottom of the pieced unit from Step 2. Set aside. (Figure C)

4. Sew 1A, 3A, 1B, and 5A together, matching the long sides. Sew 6A to the right side of the pieced unit. (Figure D)

5. Sew the unit from Step 4 to the pieced unit from Step 3. Set aside. (Figure E)

6. Sew 5B to 1C, matching the long sides. Sew 6B to the right side of the pieced unit. Set aside. (Figure F)

7. Sew 1G, 4B, 1K, and 2C together, matching the 13″ sides. Sew 5D to the top. (Figure G)

Figure H

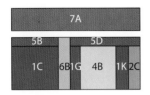

Figure I

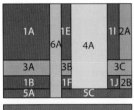

Figure J

8. Sew the Step 7 unit to the right side of the pieced unit from Step 6. (Figure H)

9. Sew 7A to the top of the pieced Step 8 unit. (Figure I)

10. Sew the pieced unit from Step 9 to the bottom of the Step 5 unit. Set aside. (Figure J)

11. Sew together 2E, 3D, 2F, 5E, 7B, 5F, and 2G, matching the 18¼˝ sides. Sew 8A to the left side of the unit. (Figure K)

12. Sew the Step 11 unit to the right side of the pieced unit from Step 10. Set aside. (Figure L)

13. Sew together 1D, 6C, 1H, 4C, 1L, 2D, 8B, and 2H, matching the 18¼˝ sides. Sew 9A to the top. (Figure M)

14. Finish the quilt back by sewing the Step 13 unit to the bottom of the pieced unit from Step 12. (Figure N)

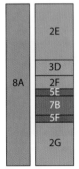

Figure K

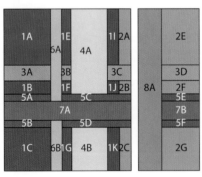

Figure L

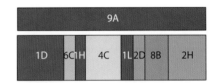

Figure M

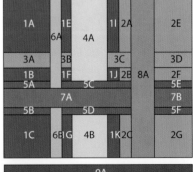

Figure N

Finishing the Quilt

Refer to Construction Basics (pages 132–141) for details on sandwiching, quilting, and binding your project.

Alternate Ideas

make it with two colors

Simplify your fabric choices by using prints and solids in just two colors. For this block, I used orange fabrics for all the vertical strips (Fabrics 1, 2, 4, 6, and 8) and blue fabrics for all the horizontal strips (Fabrics 3, 5, 7, and 9). To add interest, I included one orange print with a little blue.

make it bold

Black-and-white prints always make a statement. Combine that with vibrant violet solids for a block that packs a big visual punch. To balance the bolder fabrics, I used more somber charcoal and gray solids for the background (Fabrics 1 and 2). I also played with the fabric formula, using black-and-white prints and violet solids for both horizontal and vertical stripes.

Roller Rink

Finished block: 4″ × 16″   **Finished quilt:** 52″ × 80″   *Made and machine quilted by Elizabeth Hartman*

A four-step value scale in rich reds is paired with light and dark neutral frames to create a quilt that's full of energy. The piecing may give the illusion of waves and curves, but it's all sewn with straight seams.

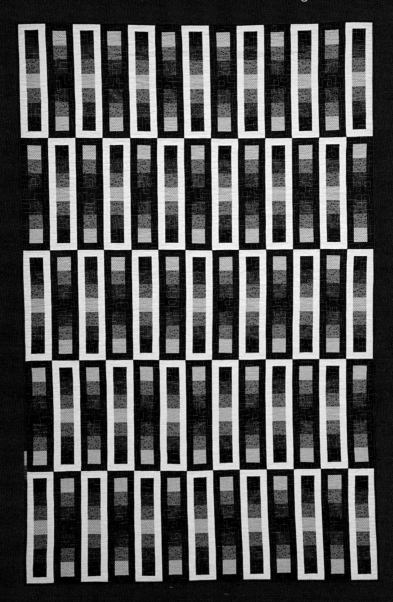

Selecting the Fabric

I started by selecting four monochromatic red print fabrics in four different values, from a light salmon to a deep scarlet. I looked for a group of prints that would create a smooth four-step value scale, with none of the prints sticking out more than the others. Then, for the quilt back, I chose four solid fabrics that match the four print fabrics.

I wanted my neutral solid sashing fabrics to complement the warmth of all the rich reds, so I chose a creamy off-white for my light neutral and a rich chocolate brown for my dark neutral. Refer to Fabric and Design Vocabulary (page 120) for more about fabric selection.

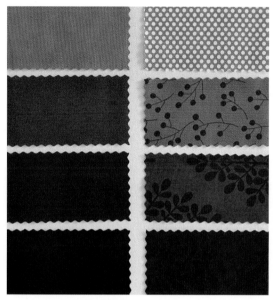

My fabric choices for Roller Rink

materials

Yardages are based on fabric that is at least 40″ wide, unless otherwise noted.

note — Fabrics are labeled as Values 1–4, with 1 being the lightest and 4 being the darkest.

¾ yard *each* of Value 1 and Value 4 monochromatic print fabric

1 yard *each* of Value 2 and Value 3 monochromatic print fabric

2½ yards *each* of light neutral and dark neutral solid sashing fabric

1¼ yards *each* of Value 1 and Value 4 solid fabric for quilt back

1 yard *each* of Value 2 and Value 3 solid fabric for quilt back

⅝ yard binding fabric

56″ × 84″ batting

cutting instructions

MONOCHROMATIC PRINT FABRICS,
FOR BLOCKS:

- From *each* Value 1 and Value 4 print fabric, cut 9 strips 2½" × width of fabric.

- From *each* Value 2 and Value 3 print fabric, cut 12 strips 2½" × width of fabric.

LIGHT NEUTRAL SOLID SASHING FABRIC,
FOR LIGHT BLOCKS:

Cut:

- 4 strips 14½" × width of fabric; subcut into 86 pieces 1½" × 14½"

- 4 strips 4½" × width of fabric; subcut into 86 pieces 1½" × 4½"

- 1 strip 4½" × width of fabric; subcut into 1 piece 16½" × 4½" for the quilt back

DARK NEUTRAL SOLID SASHING FABRIC,
FOR DARK BLOCKS:

Cut:

- 4 strips 16½" × width of fabric; subcut into 84 pieces 1½" × 16½"

- 4 strips 2½" × width of fabric; subcut into 84 pieces 1½" × 2½"

- 1 strip 4½" × width of fabric; subcut into 1 piece 16½" × 4½" for the quilt back

SOLID QUILT BACK FABRICS:

From *each* Value 1 and Value 4 solid fabric, cut:

- 1 strip 24½" × width of fabric; trim to 28½" × 24½"

- 1 strip 16½" × width of fabric; trim to 24½" × 16½"

From *each* Value 2 and Value 3 solid fabric, cut:

- 1 strip 20½" × width of fabric; trim to 36½" × 20½"

- 1 strip 8½" × width of fabric; trim to 20½" × 8½"

BINDING FABRIC:

- Cut 7 strips 2½" × width of fabric.

Making the Blocks

All seam allowances are ¼", and all seams are pressed open unless otherwise noted.

Dark and light blocks

Light Blocks

1. Sew 7 of the 2½" print fabric strips together in the following order, matching the long sides: Value 4, Value 3, Value 2, Value 1, Value 2, Value 3, and Value 4. Repeat to make a total of 3 identical strip sets.

2. Subcut the strip sets into a total of 43 pieced units, each 2½″ × 14½″.

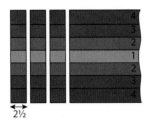

3. Sew 1½″ × 14½″ pieces of light solid sashing fabric to the left and right sides of each unit from Step 2.

4. Finish each block by sewing 1½″ × 4½″ pieces of light solid sashing fabric to the top and bottom.

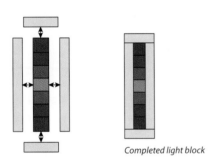

Completed light block

Dark Blocks

1. Sew 7 of the 2½″ print fabric strips together in the following order, matching the long sides: Value 1, Value 2, Value 3, Value 4, Value 3, Value 2, and Value 1. Repeat to make a total of 3 identical strip sets.

2. Subcut the strip sets into 42 pieced units, each 2½″ × 14½″.

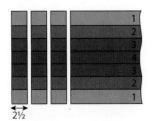

3. Sew 1½″ × 2½″ pieces of dark solid sashing fabric to the top and bottom of each unit from Step 2.

4. Finish each block by sewing a 1½″ × 16½″ piece of dark solid sashing fabric to each side.

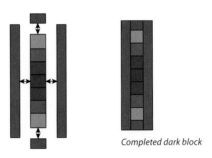

Completed dark block

Making the Quilt Top

1. Arrange the blocks in 5 rows of 13 blocks each, alternating light and dark blocks in a checkerboard pattern. Rows 1, 3, and 5 should start and end with a light block. Rows 2 and 4 should start and end with a dark block. Sew the blocks into rows.

2. Sew the 5 rows together, matching the seams where the blocks meet.

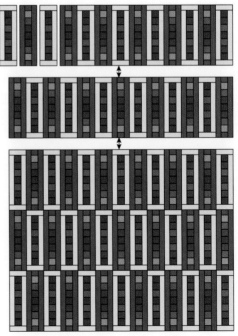

Quilt top assembly diagram

Making the Quilt Back

Refer to the quilt back assembly diagram on page 22.

Back Unit 1

1. Starting with a light block, sew together 3 light and 2 dark blocks, alternating between light and dark and matching the long sides. Sew the 4½″ × 16½″ piece of light neutral solid fabric to the bottom of the stack to create a 16½″ × 24½″ unit.

2. Sew the blocks into rows, and then sew the 24½″ × 28½″ piece of Value 1 solid fabric to the right side of the stack unit and the 24½″ × 16½″ piece to the left.

Back Unit 2

1. Starting with a dark block, sew together 3 dark and 2 light blocks, alternating between light and dark and matching the long sides to create a 16½″ × 20½″ horizontally stacked unit.

2. Sew the 20½″ × 8½″ piece of Value 2 solid fabric to the right side of the pieced stack and the 20½″ × 36½″ piece to the left.

Back Unit 3

1. Starting with a light block, sew together 3 light and 2 dark blocks, alternating between light and dark and matching the long sides to create a 16½″ × 20½″ horizontally stacked unit.

2. Sew the 20½″ × 36½″ piece of Value 3 solid fabric to the right side of the stack and the 20½″ × 8½″ piece to the left.

Back Unit 4

1. Starting with a dark block, sew together 3 dark and 2 light blocks, alternating between light and dark and matching the long sides. Sew the 4½″ × 16½″ piece of dark neutral solid fabric to the top of the stack to create a 16½″ × 24½″ unit.

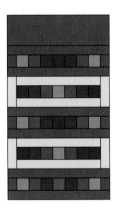

2. Sew the 24½″ × 16½″ piece of Value 4 fabric to the right side of the stack and the 24½″ × 28½″ piece to the left.

Finishing the Quilt Back

Sew together the 4 back units in order of value, starting with the darkest unit at the top and working your way to the lightest unit at the bottom.

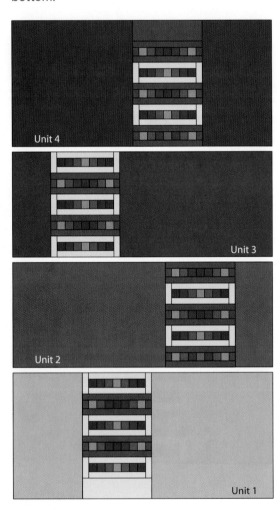

Quilt back assembly diagram

Finishing the Quilt

Refer to Construction Basics (pages 132–141) for details on sandwiching, quilting, and binding your quilt.

Alternate Ideas

make it with solids

For a simpler look, substitute four solid fabrics for the four monochromatic print fabrics. Sashing half the blocks in hot pink adds a pop of color to this all-gray value scale.

make it scrappy

All the tiny squares make this a perfect scrap-busting project. Instead of strip piecing, make each block with 7 different 2½″ × 2½″ squares. If you want to stick with the value scale concept, you'll need 127 squares of Value 1, 128 squares of Value 4, and 170 squares *each* of Values 2 and 3. Or you can just sort your favorite scraps into sets of 7, as I've done here, grouping them by color. For a quilt like this, you'll need 85 sets of 7 squares (595 squares in all).

Glam Garlands

Finished small block: 3″ × 3½″   **Finished medium block:** 4″ × 4½″   **Finished large block:** 5″ × 5½″

Finished quilt: 49″ × 68″   *Made and machine quilted by Elizabeth Hartman*

A relaxed piecing technique results in slightly different, slightly wonky blocks that resemble paper garlands swaying in the breeze. On the quilt back, three large blocks combine the fabrics used for each of the three garland colors

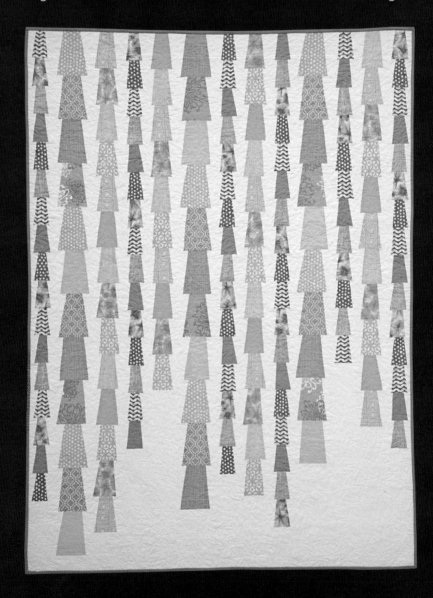

Selecting the Fabric

Three distinct color groups are used to make this quilt. Each group includes one solid and four print fabrics. The fabrics in a group don't all have to be exactly the same hue, but they should be similar enough that they will collectively read as a single color.

For my groups, I chose gold, citrine, and gray. To make sure they would read as distinct groups, I made sure to pick warm, sunny golds and cool, acidy citrines. The bright colors stand out against a white background, while a subtle gray background adds a slightly different look to the quilt back.

Refer to Fabric and Design Vocabulary (page 120) for more about fabric selection.

My fabric choices for Glam Garlands

materials

Yardages are based on fabric that is at least 40″ wide, unless otherwise noted.

½ yard gold solid fabric

½ yard *each* of 4 different gold print fabrics

½ yard citrine solid fabric

½ yard *each* of 4 different citrine print fabrics

½ yard gray solid fabric

½ yard *each* of 4 different gray print fabrics

4 yards light neutral solid for quilt top background

3⅛ yards contrasting solid for quilt back

⅝ yard binding fabric

53″ × 72″ batting

Stick-on labels

cutting instructions

GOLD FABRICS, FOR LARGE BLOCK BASES:

From the solid fabric and 2 print fabrics,
cut each into:

- 2 strips 6″ × width of fabric; subcut
  into 12 large block bases 5½″ × 6″

From the remaining 2 print fabrics, cut each into:

- 2 strips 6″ × width of fabric; subcut
  into 11 large block bases 5½″ × 6″

*There should now be a total of 58 large block bases.
Set aside 5 cut pieces from each fabric (25 total) and
any cutting scraps to use for the quilt back blocks.*

CITRINE FABRICS, FOR MEDIUM BLOCK BASES:

From the solid fabric and 2 print fabrics,
cut each into:

- 2 strips 5″ × width of fabric; subcut into
  15 medium block bases 4½″ × 5″

From the remaining 2 print fabrics, cut each into:

- 2 strips 5″ × width of fabric; subcut into
  14 medium block bases 4½″ × 5″

*There should now be a total of 73 medium block
bases. Set aside 5 cut pieces from each fabric
(25 total) and any cutting scraps to use for the
quilt back blocks.*

GRAY FABRICS, FOR SMALL BLOCK BASES:

From the solid fabric and 2 print fabrics,
cut each into:

- 3 strips 4″ × width of fabric; subcut
  into 24 small block bases 3½″ × 4″

From the remaining 2 print fabrics, cut each into:

- 3 strips 4″ × width of fabric; subcut
  into 23 small block bases 3½″ × 4″

*There should now be a total of 118 small block
bases. Set aside 5 cut pieces from each fabric
(25 total) and any cutting scraps to use for the
quilt back blocks.*

LIGHT NEUTRAL SOLID BACKGROUND FABRIC:

Cut:

- 4 strips 7″ × width of fabric; subcut
  into 66 large sashing pieces 2″ × 7″

- 5 strips 6″ × width of fabric; subcut into
  96 medium sashing pieces 1¾″ × 6″

- 8 strips 5″ × width of fabric; subcut into
  186 small sashing pieces 1½″ × 5″

- 7 strips 1½″ × width of fabric; subcut into:

  2 pieces 10½″ × 1½″ and 2 pieces
  16½″ × 1½″ for small back block sashing

  2 pieces 14½″ × 1½″ and 2 pieces 21½″ × 1½″
  for medium back block sashing

  2 pieces 16½″ × 1½″ and 2 pieces
  25½″ × 1½″ for large back block sashing

*Note: Each of the following pieces will be used at
the bottom of a column of blocks. Label each with
the number in parentheses.*

- 1 strip 5½″ × width of fabric; subcut into:

  1 piece 13½″ × 5½″ (10)

  1 piece 8″ × 5½″ (6)

  1 piece 2½″ × 5½″ (2)

- 2 strips 4½″ × width of fabric; subcut into:

  1 piece 23½″ × 4½″ (5)

  1 piece 10″ × 4½″ (8)

  1 piece 19″ × 4½″ (12)

  1 piece 5½″ × 4½″ (3)

CONTINUED ON PAGE 28

- 3 strips 3½" × width of fabric; subcut into:

  1 piece 26½" × 3½" (11)

  1 piece 16" × 3½" (4)

  1 piece 16" × 3½" (13)

  1 piece 12½" × 3½" (7)

  1 piece 9" × 3½" (1)

  1 piece 5½" × 3½" (9)

CONTRASTING SOLID QUILT BACK FABRIC:

Note: Label the quilt back pieces with the letters indicated in parentheses.

Cut:

- 1 strip 32½" × width of fabric; subcut into:

  1 piece 11½" × 32½" (A)

  1 piece 21½" × 32½" (F)

  1 piece 3½" × 32½" (D)

- 2 strips 25½" × width of fabric; subcut into:

  1 piece 39½" × 25½" (J)

  1 piece 16½" × 25½" (G)

  1 piece 14½" × 25½" (E)

- 1 strip 21½" × width of fabric; subcut into:

  1 piece 7½" × 21½" (I)

  1 piece 2½" × 21½" (H)

From the remaining fabric, cut:

- 1 piece 16½" × remaining length; subcut into:

  1 piece 12½" × 16½" (C)

  1 piece 8½" × 16½" (B)

BINDING FABRIC:

- Cut 7 strips 2½" × width of fabric.

Making the Blocks

All seam allowances are ¼", and all seams are pressed open unless otherwise noted.

Large Blocks

Each large block will be made from 1 large (5½″ × 6″) gold block base and 2 large (2″ × 7″) light neutral block sashing pieces. The idea is to piece these blocks in a semi-improvisational style, without measuring. The resulting blocks will all be slightly different, giving them the look of paper garlands swaying in the breeze when they are pieced together.

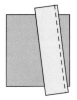

Figure A

1. With right sides together, place a sashing piece on top of a block base at a slight angle. Place the sashing close enough to the edge that, once sewn to the block base, it can be folded back to cover the edge of the block base. Sew the sashing to the base ¼″ from the outside edge of the sashing. (Figure A)

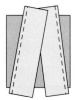

Figure B

2. Place a second piece of sashing on top of the block base, mirroring the placement of the first piece to create a tapered bell shape. Sew the sashing to the base ¼″ from the outside edge of the sashing, being careful not to catch the first sashing piece in the seam. (Figure B)

3. Trim away the excess fabric from the block base, using the seam allowances as a guide. Press the seams open. (Figure C)

Figure C

4. Trim the finished block to 5½″ × 6″. (Figure D)

5. Repeat Steps 1–4 to create 33 large blocks.

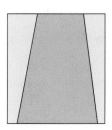

Medium Blocks

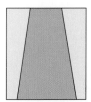

Repeat Large Blocks, Steps 1–3, using the medium 4½″ × 5″ citrine block bases and the 1¾″ × 6″ medium light neutral sashing to create 48 medium blocks. Trim to measure 4½″ × 5″.

Figure D

Small Blocks

Repeat Large Blocks, Steps 1–3, using the small 3½″ × 4″ gray block bases and the 1½″ × 5″ small light neutral sashing to create 93 small blocks. Trim to measure 3½″ × 4″.

Making the Quilt Top

1. Sew the blocks into columns along the short sides, as listed (below) and as shown in the quilt top assembly diagram (lower right), with the wider base of the bell shape at the bottom edge. For each column, intermix the solid and print block base fabrics in a pleasing order. Sew the designated light neutral solid background piece to the bottom of each pieced column.

Column 1: Sew together 17 small gray blocks. Sew the 9″ × 3½″ solid piece (1) to the bottom of the column.

Column 2: Sew together 12 large gold blocks. Sew the 2½″ × 5½″ solid piece (2) to the bottom of the column.

Column 3: Sew together 14 medium citrine blocks. Sew the 5½″ × 4½″ solid piece (3) to the bottom of the column.

Column 4: Sew together 15 small gray blocks. Sew the 16″ × 3½″ solid piece (4) to the bottom.

Column 5: Sew together 10 medium citrine blocks. Sew the 23½″ × 4½″ solid piece (5) to the bottom of the column.

Column 6: Sew together 11 large gold blocks. Sew the 8″ × 5½″ solid piece (6) to the bottom of the column.

Column 7: Sew together 16 small gray blocks. Sew the 12½″ × 3½″ solid piece (7) to the bottom of the column.

Column 8: Sew together 13 medium citrine blocks. Sew the 10″ × 4½″ solid piece (8) to the bottom of the column.

Column 9: Sew together 18 small gray blocks. Sew the 5½″ × 3½″ solid piece (9) to the bottom of the column.

Column 10: Sew together 10 large gold blocks. Sew the 13½″ × 5½″ solid piece (10) to the bottom of the column.

Column 11: Sew together 12 small gray blocks. Sew the 26½″ × 3½″ solid piece (11) to the bottom of the column.

Column 12: Sew together 11 medium citrine blocks. Sew the 19″ × 4½″ solid piece (12) to the bottom of the column.

Column 13: Sew together 15 small gray blocks. Sew the 16″ × 3½″ solid piece (13) to the bottom of the column.

2. Sew the columns together in order, 1–13, to complete the quilt top.

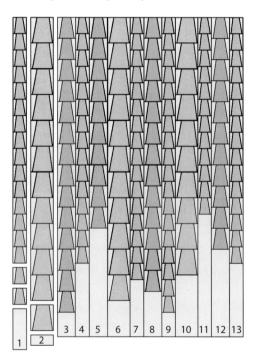

Quilt top assembly diagram

Making the Quilt Back

Large Back Block

1. Divide the 25 remaining large 5½" × 6" gold block bases into 5 sets, each including 1 piece from each of the 5 fabrics.

2. Arrange the first set of block bases in a column, matching the 5½" sides.

3. Select a block base from the second set and cut it in half, creating 2 pieces 3" × 5½". Arrange the second set of pieces in a column alongside the first column, placing the smaller cut pieces at the top and bottom of the arrangement.

4. Repeat Steps 2 and 3 to create a third column that has 5 whole block bases and a fourth column that has 4 whole block bases and 1 halved block base for the top and bottom. Repeat Step 2 to create a fifth column with 5 whole block bases. (Figure A)

5. Stitch the pieces in each column together, sewing them at slightly wonky angles. Be sure to alternate the direction of subsequent angles to ensure that the column will be balanced, rather than leaning to one side. Trim the seam allowances to ¼" and press the seams open. (Figure B)

6. Trim to straighten the sides of each column, again using slightly wonky angles and making sure to alternate the angles from one column to the next to create balance. (Figure C)

7. Sew the 5 columns together, offsetting the block seams between adjacent columns, like bricks laid in a wall. Square up the block to 16½" × 23½". (If your block is too small to be squared up to this size, just add scrap fabric. Don't worry—the improvisational piecing will enhance the look of your project!)

8. Sew the 16½" × 1½" background solid strips to the top and bottom of the block. Sew a 25½" × 1½" background solid strip to each side. (Figure D)

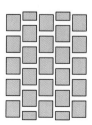

Figure A   **Figure B**   **Figure C**   **Figure D**

Medium Back Block

Follow the Large Back Block steps (page 31) but with these exceptions:

- Use the remaining medium citrine 4½″ × 5″ block bases. Arrange and sew them along the 4½″ sides.

- When cutting the block bases in half for Columns 2 and 4 (Steps 3 and 4), the resulting pieces will be 2½″ × 4½″.

- In Step 7, square up the block to 14½″ × 19½″.

- In Step 8, sew the 14½″ × 1½″ background solid strips to the top and bottom of the block. Sew the 21½″ × 1½″ background solid strips to the 2 sides.

Small Back Block

Follow the Large Back Block steps (page 31) but with these exceptions:

- Use the remaining small gray 3½″ × 4″ block bases. Arrange and sew them along the 3½″ sides.

- When cutting the block bases in half for Columns 2 and 4 (Steps 3 and 4), the resulting pieces will be 2″ × 3½″.

- In Step 7, square up the block to 10½″ × 14½″.

- In Step 8, sew the 10½″ × 1½″ solid strips to the top and bottom of the block. Sew the 16½″ × 1½″ solid strips to the 2 sides.

Finishing the Quilt Back

Refer to the quilt back assembly diagram (below).

1. Sew quilt back piece B to the left side of the small gray quilt back block and piece C to the right side, matching the 16½″ sides. Sew quilt back piece A to the top and piece D to the bottom. Set aside.

2. Sew quilt back piece E to the left side of the large gold quilt back block, matching the 25½″ sides. Sew piece F to the bottom.

3. Sew the small back block unit from Step 1 to the top of the large back block unit from Step 2 to create the left side of the quilt back. Set aside.

4. Sew quilt back piece H to the left side of the medium citrine quilt back block and piece I to the right side, matching the 21½″ sides. Sew quilt back piece G to the top and piece J to the bottom to create the right side of the quilt back.

5. Finish the quilt back by sewing the left and right sides together.

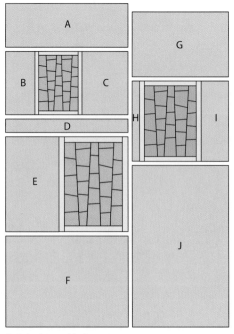

Quilt back assembly diagram

Finishing the Quilt

Refer to Construction Basics (pages 132–141) for details on sandwiching, quilting, and binding your project.

Alternate Ideas

make it bold

Using a dark chocolate brown as the background fabric really sets off the teal and aqua prints in this interpretation of the quilt pattern.

make it scrappy

Of course, you don't have to use new yardage. Dig into your scrap bin to come up with 58 pieces 5½″ × 6″ (for the large blocks), 73 pieces 4½″ × 5″ (for the medium blocks), and 118 pieces 3½″ × 4″ (for the small blocks).

Neighborhood

Finished block: 11″ × 15″   **Finished quilt:** 45″ × 60″   *Made and machine quilted by Elizabeth Hartman*

Just a few clever steps turn a collection of Log Cabin blocks into a lovely neighborhood. Framed windows allow you to add fussy-cut inhabitants to these mod houses.

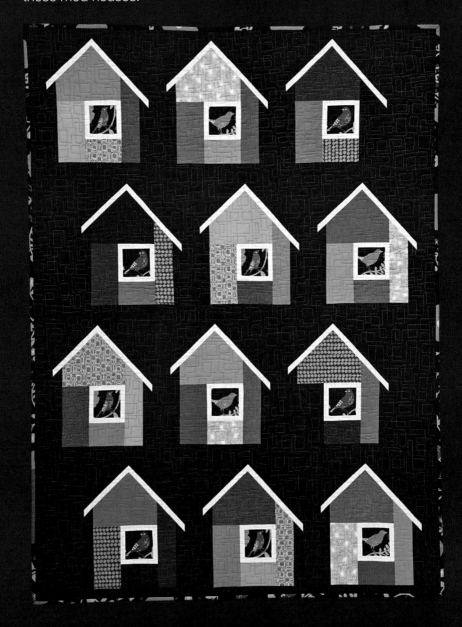

Selecting the Fabric

The first fabric I chose for this project was the bird print, from which I fussy cut the squares for the centers of the windows. Because the birds were orange, gray, and violet, I used those same colors to make my houses. I wanted to keep things simple, so I used three solid fabrics and a single monochromatic print fabric for each color group. The mahogany background and soft white window frames and rooftops create lots of contrast with the bright colors, counteracting a little of the sweetness inherent in picture blocks like this.

Refer to Fabric and Design Vocabulary (page 120) for more about fabric selection.

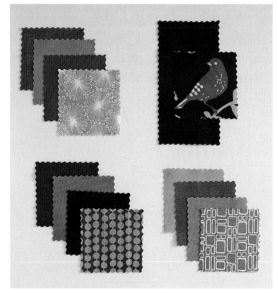

My fabric choices for Neighborhood

materials

Yardages are based on fabric that is at least 40˝ wide, unless otherwise noted. Fat quarters should measure at least 18˝ × 21˝.

15 fussy-cut print fabric squares for windows, *each* 3½˝ × 3½˝

1 fat quarter violet print fabric

1 fat quarter *each* of 3 different violet solid fabrics

1 fat quarter gray print fabric

1 fat quarter *each* of 3 different gray solid fabrics

1 fat quarter orange print fabric

1 fat quarter *each* of 3 different orange solid fabrics

5 yards solid fabric for background, at least 42˝ wide

⅝ yard contrasting solid fabric for window frames and rooftops

½ yard binding fabric

49˝ × 64˝ batting

Translucent template plastic

cutting instructions

VIOLET, ORANGE, AND GRAY FABRICS,
FOR HOUSES:

For *each* of 12 fabrics, cut:

- 1 strip 7″ × 18″ along the shorter (18″)
  side of the fat quarter; subcut into:

  1 piece 7½″ × 7″

  1 piece 3½″ × 7″

  1 piece 3″ × 4½″

- 1 strip 2½″ × 18″; trim to 2½″ × 10″

VIOLET FABRIC, FOR QUILT BACK:

- From the print fabric, cut 1 piece 3″ × 4½″.
- From the first solid fabric, cut 1 piece 3½″ × 7″.
- From the second solid fabric,
  cut 1 piece 2½″ × 10″.
- From the third solid fabric, cut 1 piece 3″ × 7½″.

ORANGE FABRIC, FOR QUILT BACK:

- From the print fabric, cut 1 piece 7″ × 7½″.
- From the first solid fabric, cut 1 piece 2½″ × 10″.
- From the second solid fabric, cut 1 piece 3½″ × 7″.
- From the third solid fabric, cut 1 piece 3″ × 4½″.

GRAY FABRIC, FOR QUILT BACK:

- From the print fabric, cut 1 piece 2½″ × 10″.
- From the first solid fabric, cut 1 piece 3″ × 7½″.
- From the second solid fabric, cut 1 piece 3″ × 4½″.
- From the third solid fabric, cut 1 piece 3½″ × 7″.

BACKGROUND SOLID FABRIC:

- Cut 8 strips 1½″ × width of fabric—reserve
  2 strips for the quilt back block; subcut
  the remaining 6 strips into 24 pieces
  10½″ × 1½″ for the quilt blocks.
- Cut 2 strips 9″ x width of fabric, subcut
  into 7 squares 9″ x 9″ for triangle B.

From the remaining fabric, cut 2 equal halves,
each about 72″ (2 yards) long.

From the first piece of 72″-long fabric, cut:

- 1 piece 12½″ × length of fabric (72″) for
  the quilt back; trim to 12½″ × 68½″
- 1 piece 11½″ × length of fabric (72″); subcut into:

  1 piece 24½″ × 11½″ for the quilt back

  1 piece 12½″ × 11½″ for the quilt back

  12 pieces 1½″ × 11½″ for the blocks

- 1 piece 15½″ × length of fabric (72″) for
  the quilt top sashing; subcut into:

  4 pieces 6½″ × 15½″

  12 pieces 2½″ × 15½″

From the second piece of 72″-long fabric, cut:

- 1 piece 30½″ × length of fabric (72″) for
  the quilt back; trim to 30½″ × 68½″
- 7 squares 7½″ × 7½″ for triangle C

  Cut each 9″ (B) and 7½″ (C) square in half
  diagonally to make 13 right triangles in
  each size for the quilt blocks. (You will
  have 1 extra triangle in each size.)

CONTRASTING SOLID FABRIC:

Cut:

- 8 strips 1″ × width of fabric for rooftops; subcut into a total of:

  13 pieces 9″ × 1″

  13 pieces 11″ × 1″

- 8 strips 1″ × width of fabric—set aside
  for chain piecing the window frames

BINDING FABRIC:

- Cut 6 strips 2½″ × width of fabric.

Making the Blocks

All seam allowances are ¼˝, and all seams are pressed open unless otherwise noted.

Windows

Chain piece the top of the fussy-cut window squares along the edges of 2 contrasting solid 1˝ × width of fabric strips, right sides facing. Press and trim the contrasting strips even with the squares. Repeat for the bottom edge and both sides to create 15 framed 4½˝ × 4½˝ windows. Set aside 3 of the windows for the quilt back.

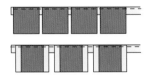

Houses

Divide the house fabric pieces cut from the 3 fabric colors into 12 matching color sets (4 of each color). Each set will have a total of 4 matching color pieces, 1 of each size and

fabric. Sew each set around a window, in the manner of a scrappy Log Cabin block, matching the similar-size sides, in this order:

1. Sew the 3˝ × 4½˝ piece to the bottom of the window (1).

2. Sew the 3½˝ × 7˝ piece to the left side (2).

3. Sew the 7½˝ × 7˝ piece to the top (3).

4. Sew the 2½˝ × 10˝ piece to the bottom right side (4).

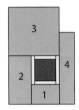

5. Sew 1½˝ × 10˝ pieces of background solid fabric to the sides of each block.

6. Sew a 1½˝ × 11½˝ piece of background solid fabric to the bottom of each block.

Roofs

1. Transfer the roof template pattern (pullout page P1) onto the translucent template plastic. Refer to Making Templates (page 124). Place your template on a quilt block, matching the window markings on the template to the pieced window on the quilt block. Using the template as a guide, cut the top of the block to resemble a peaked roof. (Figure A)

2. Sew an 11˝ × 1˝ piece of contrasting solid fabric to the right side of the rooftop. Press the seam and trim away the excess fabric to line up with the side of the block.

3. Sew a 9˝ × 1˝ piece of contrasting solid fabric to the left side of each rooftop. Press the seam and trim away the excess fabric to line up with the side of the block. (Figure B)

4. Sew a 9″ triangle B of background fabric to the right side of the rooftop, matching the long (bias) side of the triangle to the top of the roof. Press the seam and trim the triangle to match the angle of the left side of the roof.

5. Sew a 7½″ triangle C of contrasting solid fabric to the left side of the rooftop, matching the long (bias) side of the triangle to the top of the roof. (Figure C)

6. Trim the finished block to 11½″ × 15½″. (Figure D)

7. Repeat Steps 1–6 to make a total of 12 blocks (4 blocks in each of the 3 colors).

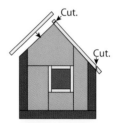

Figure B

Making the Quilt Top

Refer to quilt top assembly diagram (below).

1. Arrange the quilt blocks in 4 rows of 3 blocks each.

2. Sew together the blocks in Rows 1 and 3, adding a 2½″ × 15½″ piece of solid sashing before each block and placing a 6½″ × 15½″ piece at the end of each row.

3. Sew together the blocks in Rows 2 and 4, starting each row with a 6½″ × 15½″ solid piece and adding a 2½″ × 15½″ piece after each block.

Figure C

4. Sew the 4 rows together to finish the quilt top.

Figure D

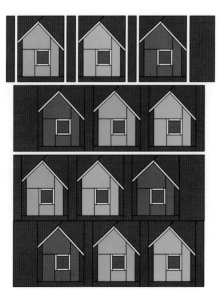

Quilt top assembly diagram

Making the Quilt Back

Back Block

Use the remaining 3 windows and 3 sets of 4 orange, violet, and gray pieces to make a 3-story house block for the quilt back.

1. Sew the 4 orange pieces around a window, the same as for the quilt top houses (page 38).

2. Sew the 3″ × 4½″ gray piece to the bottom of a window. Sew the 3½″ × 7″ piece to the right side and the 3″ × 7½″ piece to the top. Sew the 2½″ × 10″ piece to the left side, noting that this piece is slightly longer than needed. Trim the block to 9½″ × 9½″ square.

3. Sew the 4 violet pieces around a window the same way you did for the quilt top houses (page 38), but substituting the 3″ × 7½″ piece for the 7″ × 7½″ top piece. Note that the 2½″ × 10″ is slightly longer than needed. Trim the block to 9½″ × 9½″ square.

4. Sew the 3 "stories" together, placing orange on top, gray in the middle, and violet on the bottom.

5. Sew a reserved piece of 1½″ × width of fabric background solid to each side of the block, trimming away any excess fabric. (Figure A)

6. Add a roof to the top of the orange block, using the same template and steps used on the other quilt blocks (page 38). Trim the finished block to 11½″ × 32½″. (Figure B)

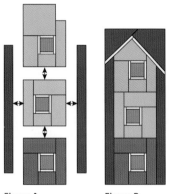

Figure A   **Figure B**

Finishing the Quilt Back

Sew the 24½″ × 11½″ piece to the top of the back block and the 12½″ × 11½″ piece to the bottom. Sew the 30½″ × 68½″ piece to the left and the 12½″ × 68½″ piece to the right to complete the quilt back.

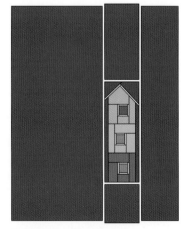

Quilt back assembly diagram

Finishing the Quilt

*Refer to Construction Basics (pages 132–141) for details
on sandwiching, quilting, and binding your project.*

Alternate Ideas

make it different

Instead of a dark background with lighter
window frames and roofs, try a light background with dark accents.

make it wild

Spice things up by building your houses out of
bold prints. Use a coordinating solid fabric in
each window for a pop of color that will help
focus and unify all the wild prints.

Rapid City

Finished block: 15″ × 20″   **Finished quilt:** 64″ × 84″   *Made and machine quilted by Elizabeth Hartman*

Inspired by the fabulous hideout adjacent to Mount Rushmore in the classic movie *North by Northwest,* this quilt features a scattering of stylized log cabins and trees.

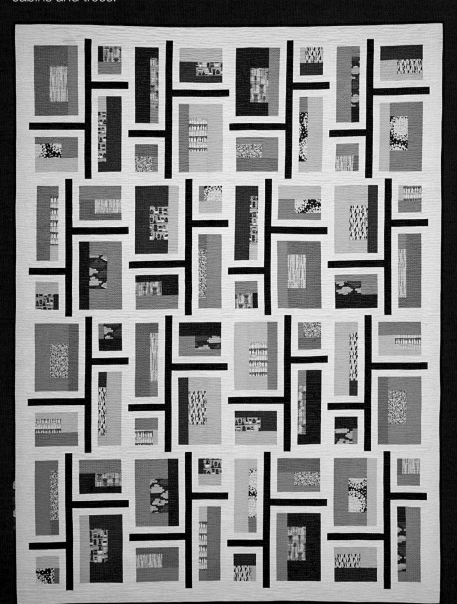

Selecting the Fabric

The blocks for this quilt are made with eight print fabrics and eight solids—I started with coordinating prints and chose solid-colored fabric that I thought would show them off. The prints are limited to a small portion of each block, set off by the surrounding solid fabrics, making this quilt the perfect showcase for small cuts of those favorite print fabrics that you really want to shine.

You don't need to find solid colors that are exactly the same as the ones in the print fabrics; colors that are a little bit different in value or intensity often make for more interesting compositions. In keeping with my goal of highlighting the print fabrics and solid colors, I chose a pure white solid for the background and an almost-black solid for the trees (crossbars).

Refer to Fabric and Design Vocabulary (page 120) for more about fabric selection.

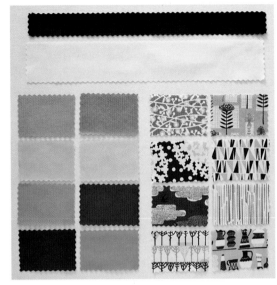

My fabric choices for Rapid City

materials

Yardages are based on fabric that is at least 40˝ wide, unless otherwise noted.

¼ yard *each* of 8 coordinating print fabrics for blocks

½ yard *each* of 8 coordinating solid fabrics for blocks, at least 42˝ wide

4 yards light neutral background solid

1¼ yards dark solid fabric for trees, at least 42˝ wide

4 yards solid fabric for quilt back, at least 42˝ wide

⅝ yard binding fabric

68˝ × 88˝ batting

20 plastic sandwich bags

Stick-on labels

cutting instructions

note This quilt uses many different pieces, cut from lots of different fabrics. Use labeled plastic bags to keep the pieces in order while you work. Start by labeling 20 bags as follows: A, A1, A2, A3, A back, B, B1, B2, B back, C, C1, C2, C3, C back, D, D1, D2, D3, D4, and D back. Sort the pieces into the appropriate bags as you cut, as indicated by the letters in parentheses in the cutting instructions.

PRINT FABRICS:

For the quilt top blocks, from *each* of the 8 print fabrics, cut:

- 2 strips 1¾″ × *length* of fabric (about 9″); trim each to 7¾″ × 1¾″ (A)
- 2 strips 3¼″ × *length* of fabric; subcut into:

  2 pieces 2¾″ × 3¼″ (B)

  2 pieces 5½″ × 3¼″ (D)
- 1 strip 4½″ × *length* of fabric; subcut into 2 pieces 2½″ × 4½″ (C)

For the quilt back block, cut each of the following pieces from a *different* print fabric:

- 1 piece 3″ × 15″ (A back)
- 1 piece 5″ × 6″ (B back)
- 1 piece 4½″ × 8½″ (C back)
- 1 piece 6″ × 10½″ (D back)

COORDINATING SOLID FABRICS:

For the quilt blocks, from *each* of 8 coordinating solids, cut:

- 1 strip 2¾″ × width of fabric; subcut into:

  2 pieces 11½″ × 2¾″ (A3)

  2 pieces 1¾″ × 2¾″ (A1)

  2 pieces 1¾″ × 2″ (A2)

  2 pieces 1¼″ × 2¾″ (B1)

  2 pieces 4″ × 2¼″ (B2)

- 1 strip 3″ × width of fabric; subcut into:

  2 pieces 3½″ × 3″ (C2)

  2 pieces 7″ × 2½″ (C3)

  2 pieces 4½″ × 1½″ (C1)
- 1 strip 3¼″ × width of fabric; subcut into:

  2 pieces 2½″ × 3¼″ (D1)

  2 pieces 3½″ × 3¼″ (D2)

  2 pieces 10½″ × 2¾″ (D3)
- 1 strip 2″ × width of fabric; subcut into 2 pieces 10½″ × 2″ (D4)

For the quilt back block, use a *different* coordinating solid fabric for each of the following:

- 1 piece 3″ × 5″ (A back)
- 1 piece 3″ × 3½″ *and* 1 piece 5″ × 22½″, from the same fabric (A back)
- 1 piece 4″ × 7½″ (B back)
- 1 piece 2″ × 5″ (B back)
- 1 piece 4½″ × 13½″ (C back)
- 1 piece 5½″ × 6½″ *and* 1 piece 2½″ × 8½″, from the same fabric (C back)
- 1 piece 3½″ × 20½″ (D back)
- 1 piece 5″ × 20½″, 1 piece 6″ × 4½″, *and* 1 piece 6″ × 6½″, from the same fabric (D back)

LIGHT NEUTRAL BACKGROUND SOLID FABRIC:

Cut:

- 11 strips 1½″ × width of fabric; subcut into 32 pieces 11½″ × 1½″ (A)
- 6 strips 1½″ × width of fabric; subcut into 32 pieces 6″ × 1½″ (A)
- 11 strips 1½″ × width of fabric; subcut into 32 pieces 10½″ × 1½″ (D)
- 8 strips 1½″ × width of fabric; subcut into 32 pieces 9″ × 1½″ (D)

CONTINUED ON PAGE 46

From the remaining length of fabric, cut:

- 10 strips 2½" × *length* of remaining fabric (about 85")—set aside 4 strips for the quilt borders; subcut the rest as follows:

  From 1 strip, cut 2 pieces 40½" × 2½" (for the back block sashing).

  From 1 strip, cut 2 pieces 34½" × 2½" (for the back block sashing).

  From 1 strip, cut 2 pieces 11½" × 2½" and 2 pieces 22½" × 2½" (A back).

  From 1 strip, cut 2 pieces 11½" × 2½" and 2 pieces 8½" × 2½" (B back).

  From 1 strip, cut 2 pieces 17½" × 2½" and 2 pieces 10½" × 2½" (C back).

  From 1 strip, cut 2 pieces 17½" × 2½" and 2 pieces 20½" × 2½" (D back).

From the remaining fabric (about 16" × 85"), cut:

- 3 strips 4½" × 16" and 1 strip 1½" × 16"; subcut into 32 pieces 1½" × 4½" (B)
- 3 strips 6" × 16" and 1 strip 1½" × 16"; subcut into 32 pieces 1½" × 6" (B)
- 3 strips 5½" × 16" and 1 strip 1½" × 16"; subcut into 32 pieces 1½" × 5½" (C)
- 3 strips 9" × 16" and 2 strips 1½" × 16"; subcut into 32 pieces 1½" × 9" (C)

DARK SOLID FABRIC:

Cut:

- 1 strip 20½" × width of fabric; subcut into 16 pieces 1½" × 20½", for the block long crossbar (sashing)
- 1 strip 9" × width of fabric; subcut into 16 pieces 1½" × 9" (C)
- 1 strip 6" × width of fabric; subcut into 16 pieces 1½" × 6" (A)
- 1 strip 2½" × width of fabric; trim to 40½" × 2½", for the back block long crossbar (sashing)
- 1 strip 2½" × width of fabric; subcut into:

  1 piece 11½" × 2½" (A back)

  1 piece 17½" × 2½" (C back)

BACK FABRIC:

Cut:

- 1 strip 34½" × width of fabric; trim to 40½" × 34½"
- 1 strip 12½" × width of fabric; trim to 34½" × 12½"
- 1 strip 12½" × *length* of the remaining fabric (about 97")

  Keep the leftover fabric (approximately 29" × 97") for piecing the quilt back.

BINDING FABRIC:

- Cut 8 strips 2½" × width of fabric.

Making the Blocks

All seam allowances are ¼″, and all seams are pressed open unless otherwise noted.

Block Component A

1. Gather the bags of A, A1, A2, and A3 pieces.

2. Select a 7¾″ × 1¾″ print from bag A. Select a 1¾″ × 2¾″ solid from bag A1 and sew it to the bottom of the print piece.

3. Select a 1¾″ × 2″ piece of a different solid fabric from bag A2 and sew it to the top of the print piece.

4. Select a 2¾″ × 11½″ piece of the same solid fabric from bag A3 and sew it to the left side of the block.

5. Sew a 1½″ × 11½″ background solid piece from bag A to each side of the block.

6. Sew 1½″ × 6″ background solid pieces from bag A to the top and bottom of the block.

7. Sew a 1½″ × 6″ dark solid piece from bag A to the bottom of the block.

8. Repeat Steps 2–7 to create a total of 16 Block Component A units.

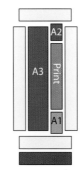

Block Component A assembly diagram

Block Component B

1. Gather the bags of B, B1, and B2 pieces.

2. Select a 2¾″ × 3¼″ print from bag B. Select a 1¼″ × 2¾″ solid from bag B1 and sew it to the right side of the print piece.

3. Select a 2¼″ × 4″ piece of a different solid from bag B2 and sew it to the top of the block.

4. Sew a 1½″ × 4½″ background solid piece from bag B to each side of the block.

5. Sew 1½″ × 6″ background solid pieces from bag B to the top and bottom of the block.

6. Repeat Steps 2–5 to create a total of 16 Block Component B units.

Block Component B assembly diagram

Block Component C

1. Gather the bags of C, C1, C2, and C3 pieces.

2. Select a 2½″ × 4½″ print from bag C. Select a 1½″ × 4½″ solid from bag C1 and sew it to the bottom of the print piece.

3. Select a 3″ × 3½″ piece of the same solid from bag C2 and sew it to the left side of the block.

4. Select a 2½″ × 7″ piece of a different solid from bag C3 and sew it to the top of the block.

5. Sew a 1½″ × 5½″ background solid piece from bag C to each side of the block.

6. Sew 1½″ × 9″ background solid pieces from bag C to the top and bottom of the block.

7. Sew a 1½″ × 9″ piece of dark solid fabric from bag C to the bottom of the block.

8. Repeat Steps 2–7 to create a total of 16 Block Component C units.

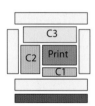

Block Component C assembly diagram

Block Component D

1. Gather the bags of D, D1, D2, D3, and D4 pieces.

2. Select a 3¼″ × 5½″ print from bag D. Select a 3¼″ × 2½″ solid from bag D1 and sew it to the top of the print piece.

3. Select a 3¼″ × 3½″ piece of the same solid from bag D2 and sew it to the bottom of the block.

4. Select a 2¾″ × 10½″ piece of the same solid from bag D3 and sew it to the right side of the block.

5. Select a 2″ × 10½″ piece of a different solid from bag D4 and sew it to the left side of the block.

6. Sew a 1½″ × 10½″ background solid from bag D to each side of the block.

7. Sew 1½″ × 9″ background solid pieces from bag D to the top and bottom of the block.

8. Repeat Steps 2–7 to create a total of 16 Block Component D units.

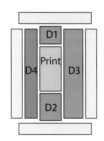

Block Component D assembly diagram

Finishing the Blocks

1. Sew each Block Component A to the top of a Block Component B.

2. Sew each Block Component C to the top of a Block Component D.

3. Sew the joined block units together with a 1½″ × 20½″ piece of dark solid fabric between them.

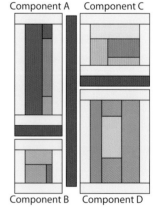

Block assembly diagram

Making the Quilt Top

1. Arrange the blocks in 4 rows of 4 blocks, rotating every other block 180° and alternating the position of each row's starting block. Sew the blocks in each row together.

2. Sew the 4 rows together.

3. Sew a 2½″ × 82″ border piece to each side of the quilt top, trimming excess fabric at the ends to match the quilt sides. Sew the remaining 2 border pieces to the top and bottom of the quilt, again trimming excess fabric to match the quilt sides.

Quilt top assembly diagram

Making the Quilt Back

1. Use the A back pieces to make a larger version of Block Component A (page 47). Sew the 3″ × 5″ solid piece to the bottom of the 3″ × 15″ print piece and the 3″ × 3½″ solid piece to the top. Sew the 5″ × 22½″ solid piece to the left side. Sew a 2½″ × 22½″ background solid piece to each side and the 2½″ × 11½″ pieces to the top and bottom. Sew the 2½″ × 11½″ dark solid piece to the bottom.

2. Use the B back pieces to make a larger version of Block Component B (page 47). Sew the 2″ × 5″ solid piece to the right side of the 5″ × 6″ print piece; then sew the 4″ × 7½″ solid piece to the top. Sew a 2½″ × 8½″ background solid piece to each side and the 2½″ × 11½″ pieces to the top and bottom.

3. Use the C back pieces to make a larger version of Block Component C (page 48). Sew the 2½˝ × 8½˝ solid piece to the bottom of the 4½˝ × 8½˝ print piece; then sew the 5½˝ × 6½˝ solid piece to the left side. Sew the 4½˝ × 13½˝ solid piece to the top. Sew a 2½˝ × 10½˝ background solid piece to each side and the 2½˝ × 17½˝ pieces to the top and bottom. Finally, sew the 2½˝ × 17½˝ dark solid piece to the bottom.

4. Use the D back pieces to make a larger version of Block Component D (page 48). Sew the 6˝ × 4½˝ solid piece to the top of the 6˝ × 10½˝ print piece and the 6˝ × 6½˝ solid piece to the bottom. Sew the 5˝ × 20½˝ solid piece to the right side and the 3½˝ × 20½˝ solid piece to the left side. Sew a 2½˝ × 20½˝ background solid piece to each side and the 2½˝ × 17½˝ pieces to the top and bottom.

5. Sew the large block components together, as in Finishing the Blocks (page 48), using the 2½˝ × 40½˝ dark solid to join the blocks.

6. Sew the 2½˝ × 40½˝ back block sashing pieces to the sides of the large block. Sew the 2½˝ × 34½˝ pieces to the top and bottom.

7. Sew the backing pieces to the top, bottom, and sides of the large block, as shown in the quilt back assembly diagram.

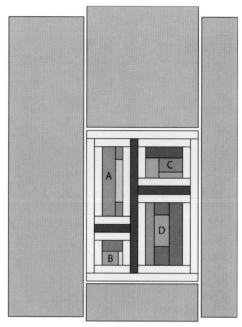

Quilt back assembly diagram

Finishing the Quilt

Refer to Construction Basics (pages 132–141) for details on sandwiching, quilting, and binding your project.

Alternate Ideas

make it scrappy

The many small pieces and the sandwich-bag organization system make this another great scrap-busting project. The chart makes it easy to substitute scraps for the 8 print and 8 coordinating solid fabrics in the pattern.

BAG	NUMBER OF PIECES	SIZE
A	16	1¾″ × 7¾″
A1	16	1¾″ × 2¾″
A2	16	1¾″ × 2″
A3	16	2¾″ × 11½″
B	16	2¾″ × 3¼″
B1	16	1¼″ × 2¾″
B2	16	2¼″ × 4″
C	16	2½″ × 4½″
C1	16	1½″ × 4½″
C2	16	3″ × 3½″
C3	16	2½″ × 7″
D	16	3¼″ × 5½″
D1	16	2½″ × 3¼″
D2	16	3¼″ × 3½″
D3	16	2¾″ × 10½″
D4	16	2″ × 10½″
BACK A	1 each	3″ × 3½″ 3″ × 5″ 3″ × 15″ 5″ × 22½″
BACK B	1 each	2″ × 5″ 4″ × 7½″ 5″ × 6″
BACK C	1 each	2½″ × 8½″ 4½″ × 8½″ 4½″ × 13½″ 5½″ × 6½″
BACK D	1 each	3½″ × 20½″ 4½″ × 6″ 5″ × 20½″ 6″ × 6½″ 6″ × 10½″

make it fussy

This is a wonderful pattern for showcasing fussy-cut print fabric.

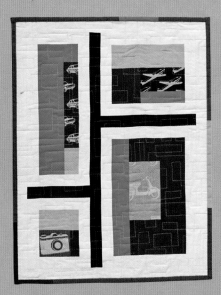

Fire Drill

Finished block: 11½″ × 19½″ diamond   **Finished quilt:** 59″ × 69″   *Made and machine quilted by Elizabeth Hartman*

If you've never pieced with diamonds, now is the time to start! Adding identical strips to both sides of a diamond-shaped base creates a beautiful pattern, full of movement, that's both sharp and wavy at the same time.

Selecting the Fabric

The fabrics for this quilt include a range of warm colors, from subtle ivory and taupe to papaya and fire orange. I chose eight print fabrics with organic patterns to counter the angular nature of the block pattern. My eight solid fabrics are, for the most part, quite a bit brighter and darker than my prints, which creates some dynamic contrast with both the prints and the ivory solid background fabric.

Refer to Fabric and Design Vocabulary (page 120) for more about fabric selection.

My fabric choices for Fire Drill

materials

Yardages are based on fabric that is at least 40˝ wide, unless otherwise noted.

⅞ yard *each* of 8 different coordinating print fabrics for blocks

⅝ yard *each* of 8 different coordinating solid fabrics for blocks

1¾ yards neutral solid background fabric for quilt top

5 yards neutral solid background fabric for quilt back

⅝ yard binding fabric

63˝ × 73˝ batting

Translucent template plastic

11 plastic sandwich bags

Water-soluble or chalk fabric marker

note

> The fabric requirements and cutting directions for the blocks allow for a few extra strips of each fabric, to give you some leeway in planning your combinations as you sew. If you prefer to cut exactly the number of strips you will need, refer to the Make It Scrappy variation (page 61).

Making the Templates

Use translucent template plastic and the patterns at the back of the book (pullout page P1) to make templates for the block base and the half-block base. Refer to Making Templates (page 124) and Cutting Template Shapes (page 129).

cutting instructions

This quilt uses many different pieces, cut from lots of different fabrics. Use labeled sandwich bags to keep them in order. Label the 11 bags as follows: A1, A2, A3, B1, B2, B3, C1, C2, C3, Back1, and Back2. Sort the pieces into the appropriate bags as you cut, as indicated by the letters in parentheses in the cutting instructions.

PRINT FABRICS, FOR BLOCKS:

From *each* of the 8 print fabrics, cut:
- 6 strips 2½″ × width of fabric; subcut into:

  3 pieces 27″ × 2½″ (B3)

  3 pieces 20″ × 2½″ (B1)
- 3 strips 3″ × width of fabric; subcut into:

  2 pieces 23″ × 3″ (A2)

  3 pieces 12½″ × 3″ (C2)

  Save the leftover fabric for the quilt back (Back2).

SOLID FABRICS, FOR BLOCKS:

From *each* of the 8 solid fabrics, cut:
- 3 strips 1½″ × width of fabric; subcut into 3 pieces 23″ × 1½″ (B2)
- 4 strips 1¾″ × width of fabric; subcut into:

  2 pieces 27″ × 1¾″ (A3)

  2 pieces 9½″ × 1¾″ (C1)

  2 pieces 16½″ × 1¾″ (A1)

  2 pieces 14½″ × 1¾″ (C3)
- 2 strips 2¼″ × width of fabric; subcut into 7 pieces 9″ × 2¼″ (Back1)

NEUTRAL SOLID BACKGROUND FABRIC:

- Use the block base template pattern to cut 33 pieces. Cut the pieces, as indicated, following the grainline.
- Use the half-block base template pattern to cut 12 pieces. Use a fabric marker or chalk to mark the straight-grain edge on each triangle.

BACK FABRIC:

- Cut 7 strips 5½″ × width of fabric; subcut into 13 pieces 18″ × 5½″ for the zigzag blocks.
- Cut the remaining fabric into 2 pieces, each 69″ long.

  Trim 1 piece to 34″ × length of fabric.

  From the second piece, cut 1 strip 15″ × length of fabric and 2 strips 12″ × length of fabric.

  Using the 60° markings on your quilting ruler, subcut the 12″ strips into a total of 13 equilateral triangles (each angle 60° and each side 12″). Mark the straight-grain edge of each triangle. For information about using the angle markings on your ruler, see Making Angled Cuts (page 129).

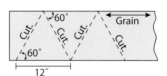

Cutting equilateral triangles

BINDING FABRIC:

- Cut 7 strips 2½″ × width of fabric.

Making the Blocks

All seam allowances are ¼˝, and all seams are pressed open unless otherwise noted.

Block A

1. Select a strip from the bag A1 pieces and cut it into a 1¾˝ × 7½˝ piece and a 1¾˝ × 9˝ piece.

2. Sew the 7½˝ strip to the top left side of a block base, lining up the end of the strip about ½˝ beyond the top center.

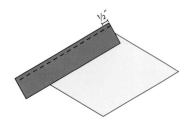

note	The angled sides of the block base can easily stretch. Use care when handling and sewing the blocks.

3. Press the seam open and trim the top corner of the block to match the top right edge of the block base.

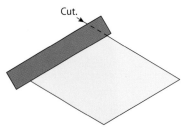

4. Sew the 9˝ strip to the top right side of the block base, lining up the end of the strip about ½˝ beyond the top center (which is now the previous strip, not the block base itself). Trim to match the top left edge of the block.

5. Select a strip from bag A2 and cut it into a 3˝ × 10˝ piece and a 3˝ × 13˝ piece. Repeat Steps 2–4 to sew the 10˝ piece to the top left and the 13˝ piece to the top right of the block, trimming to match the block edges.

6. Select a strip from bag A3 and cut it into a 1¾˝ × 13˝ piece and a 1¾˝ × 14˝ piece. Repeat Steps 2–4 to sew the 13˝ piece to the top left and the 14˝ piece to the top right, trimming to match the block edges.

7. Trim the left and right bottom edges to match the block base edges.

8. Repeat Steps 1–7 to make a total of 12 Block A units. Finished Block A should measure 10½″ from one side to the opposite parallel side. Save the leftover fabrics for making the back.

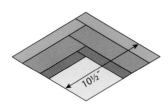

> **tip** This piecing process has you selecting strips from the sandwich bags as you sew, rather than sorting them all before you start. You can choose strips randomly or, like me, dig around a bit to find the fabric you think best complements the others in the block.

Half-Block A

1. Place a half-block base on your work surface, with one point facing left and the straight-grain edge on the right. Select a 1¾″ × 9½″ strip from the C1 bag, center it along the top edge of the block base, and sew in place. Sew on a 3″ × 12½″ strip from bag C2 and then a 1¾″ × 14½″ strip from C3, centering each strip over the previous one.

2. Trim the ends of the strips to match the edges of the base.

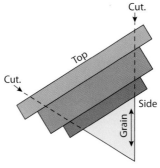

Making Half-Block A

3. Repeat Steps 1 and 2 to make a total of 6 Half-Block A units for the right side of the quilt top.

4. Arrange a half-block base piece on your work surface, with one point facing right and the straight-grain edge on the left. Sew strips from bags C1, C2, and C3 to the top of the block base, centering each subsequent strip. Trim to match the side and bottom edges of the base.

5. Repeat Step 4 to make a total of 6 Half-Block A units for the left side of the quilt top.

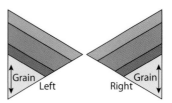

Half-Block A for left and right sides of quilt top

Block B

1. Select a strip from bag B1 and cut it into a 2½″ × 9″ piece and a 2½″ × 11″ piece. Using the same technique as for Block A, but in reverse order, sew the 9″ strip to the top *right* side of a block base. Trim to match the top left edge of the base and then sew on the 11″ piece to the left side, again trimming to match the edges.

2. Select a strip from bag B2 and cut it into a 1½˝ × 11˝ piece and a 1½˝ × 12˝ piece. Sew the 11˝ strip to the top *right* and then the 12˝ strip to the top *left* of the block, trimming the top ends of the strips to match the block edges.

3. Select a strip from bag B3 and cut it into a 2½˝ × 12½˝ piece and a 2½˝ × 14½˝ piece. Sew the 12½˝ strip to the top *right* and the 14½˝ strip to the top *left* of the block, trimming to match the block edges.

4. Trim the bottom left and bottom right block strip ends to match the block base edges.

5. Repeat Steps 1–4 to make a total of 21 Block B units.

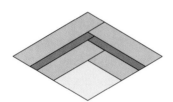

Block B

Making the Quilt Top

1. Arrange the finished blocks and half-blocks in 9 diagonal rows according to the quilt top assembly diagram (at right).

2. Sew the blocks into diagonal rows and then sew the rows together, matching the seams between blocks. At this point, the top and bottom edges of the quilt top will be zigzag-shaped.

3. Leaving as much of the blocks as possible, trim the top and bottom of the quilt top to make a rectangle approximately 59½˝ × 69½˝.

tip Joining diamonds requires a bit more effort than joining squares, but there's a simple trick to it. Use your ruler and a fabric marker to indicate the points at each corner ¼˝ in from each side, where the blocks will meet. When you sew the blocks together, simply match these dots. The blocks will be slightly offset before they are sewn; but once the seam is opened, the edges should line up perfectly.

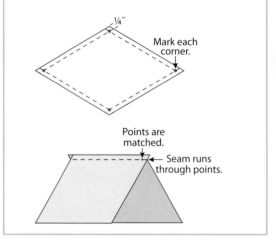

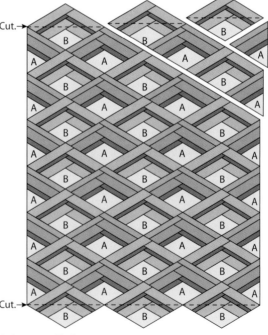

Quilt top assembly diagram

Making the Quilt Back

Zigzag Blocks

1. Use the scraps in the Back2 bag and any leftover print fabric strips from Blocks A and B to cut 39 pieces 1½″ × 9″.

2. Sew together 3 print strips from Step 1 and 4 solid 2¼″ × 9″ strips from the Back1 bag, alternating prints and solids and beginning and ending with a solid. Stagger the strips, insetting each subsequent strip 1″ from the right side of the previous one to create a pieced stack that tilts to the left.

3. Use the 60° markings on your ruler to cut the pieced stack into a 60° parallelogram that tilts to the left and measures 5½″ across parallel lines.

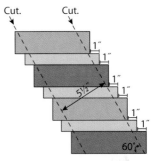

4. Repeat Steps 1–3 to create a total of 7 pieced stacks.

5. Sew a pieced stack to an 18″ × 5½″ back fabric strip, lining up the pieces as shown. Press the seams open and trim the solid back fabric to match the edges of the pieced stack, creating a diamond block measuring 10½″ from one side to the opposite parallel side.

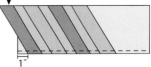

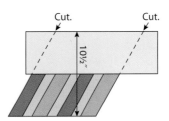

6. Repeat Step 5 to make a total of 7 blocks.

7. Sew together 3 print strips from Step 1 and 4 solid strips from the Back1 bag, alternating prints and solids and beginning and ending with a solid. This time, line up the strips 1″ from the *left* side of the previous strip to create a pieced stack that tilts to the *right*.

8. Use the 60° markings on your ruler to cut the stack into a 60° parallelogram that tilts to the *right* and measures 5½″ across.

9. Repeat Steps 7 and 8 to create a total of 6 pieced stacks.

10. Use the process from Step 5 to create 6 more blocks that will be mirror images of the 7 blocks you've already made.

Regular and mirror-image blocks

Finishing the Quilt Back

Arrange the zigzag blocks and solid triangles according to the quilt back assembly diagram (below). Sew the blocks and triangles into 8 diagonal rows and then sew the rows together to create a pieced zigzag that runs across the width of the quilt back. Sew the 34″ solid piece to the top and the 15″ solid piece to the bottom to finish the quilt back.

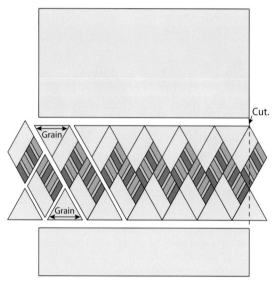

Quilt back assembly diagram

Finishing the Quilt

Refer to Construction Basics (pages 132–141) for details on sandwiching, quilting, and binding your project.

Alternate Ideas

make it cooler

Using gray print fabrics and a bold teal solid fabric for this quilt pattern creates a totally different look.

make it scrappy

Instead of cutting from new yardage, cut the print and solid fabric strips from scraps. To keep everything organized, use the pattern instructions to separate the 11 different pieces into sandwich bags. Here's what you'll need:

BAG	NUMBER OF PIECES	SIZE
A1	12 pieces	1¾″ × 16½″
A2	12 pieces	3″ × 23″
A3	12 pieces	1¾″ × 27″
B1	21 pieces	2½″ × 20″
B2	21 pieces	1½″ × 23″
B3	21 pieces	2½″ × 27″
C1	12 pieces	1¾″ × 9½″
C2	12 pieces	3″ × 12½″
C3	12 pieces	1¾″ × 14½″
BACK1	52 pieces	2¼″ × 9″
BACK2	39 pieces	1½″ × 9″

Xylophone

Finished small block: 4″ × 23″   **Finished medium block:** 6″ × 23″   **Finished large block:** 8″ × 23″

Finished quilt: 92″ × 88″   *Made and machine quilted by Elizabeth Hartman*

This project uses color-coordinated groups of fabric to create lively blocks in three different sizes. Improvisational cutting of the block units creates endless variation and ensures that no two blocks will be exactly the same. Use the leftover block units to create giant wonky stacks on the quilt back.

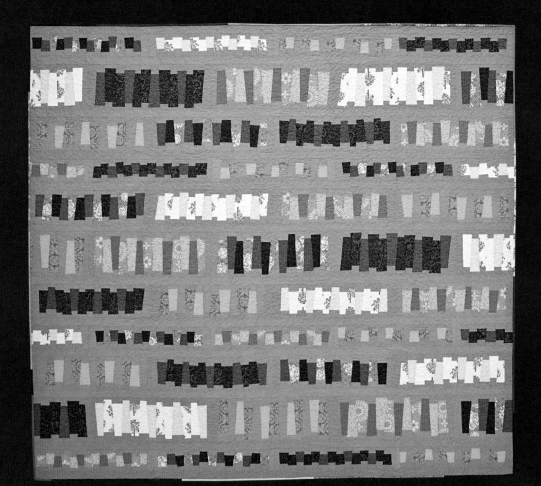

Selecting the Fabric

The blocks for this quilt are made with five different color-coordinated fabric groups, each including one solid and two print fabrics. I chose fabrics in a complementary color scheme featuring coral, green, and white. If you look carefully, you can see that some of my fabric groups are a little more closely coordinated than others. When selecting your fabrics, think about whether you'd prefer to have more solid blocks of color (like my coral, white, and avocado blocks) or more varicolored blocks (like my chartreuse and grass green blocks).

Refer to Fabric and Design Vocabulary (page 120) for more about fabric selection.

My fabric choices for Xylophone

materials

Yardages are based on fabric that is at least 40″ wide, unless otherwise noted.

⅝ yard *each* of 1 chartreuse solid fabric and 2 chartreuse print fabrics for blocks

⅝ yard *each* of 1 grass green solid fabric and 2 grass green print fabrics for blocks

⅝ yard *each* of 1 avocado solid fabric and 2 avocado print fabrics for blocks

⅝ yard *each* of 1 coral solid fabric and 2 coral print fabrics for blocks

⅝ yard *each* of 2 white print fabrics for blocks

5½ yards white solid fabric for quilt back and blocks, at least 42″ wide

12⅛ yards putty-colored solid fabric for blocks, backgrounds, and sashing

96″ × 92″ batting

Note: The scrappy binding is made from pieces of the block fabrics.

cutting instructions

BLOCK FABRICS:

From *each* of the 14 block ⅝ yard fabrics, cut:

- 1 strip 6½″ × width of fabric
  for the large blocks
- 1 strip 4½″ × width of fabric
  for the medium blocks
- 1 strip 2½″ × width of fabric
  for the small blocks
- 1 strip 2½″ × width of fabric, trimmed
  to 25½″, for the scrappy binding

WHITE SOLID FABRIC:

- For the quilt blocks, cut:

  1 strip 6½″ × width of fabric

  1 strip 4½″ × width of fabric

  1 strip 2½″ × width of fabric

- Cut the remaining fabric into 2 equal-length
  pieces about 96″ long. Trim the selvages
  from 1 piece, leaving a large quilt back panel
  approximately 42″ × 96″. From the other
  piece, cut another quilt back panel 33″ × 96″.

PUTTY SOLID FABRIC:

Cut:

- 30 strips 3½″ × width of fabric
  for the large blocks
- 30 strips 3″ × width of fabric
  for the medium blocks
- 30 strips 2½″ × width of fabric
  for the small blocks
- 2 strips 10″ × width of fabric;
  subcut into 24 pieces 3″ × 10″
  for the large blocks
- 3 strips 8″ × width of fabric;
  subcut into 32 pieces 3″ × 8″
  for the medium blocks
- 3 strips 6″ × width of fabric;
  subcut into 32 pieces 3″ × 6″
  for the small blocks
- 16 strips 2½″ × *length* of the
  remaining fabric (about 100″) for
  the top and back sashing

Making the Blocks

*All seam allowances are ¼″, and all seams are
pressed open unless otherwise noted.*

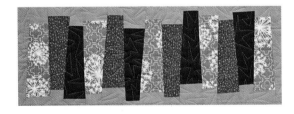

Large Blocks

1. Sew a 3½″ putty solid fabric strip to each side
of a 6½″ grass green fabric strip. Repeat with the
2 remaining 6½″ grass green strips to make a
total of 3 large grass green strip sets.

2. Use your ruler and rotary cutter to cut each
strip set into about 18–22 wedge units, tilting
the ruler back and forth at a slightly wonky
angle with each cut. Don't measure—the idea is
to end up with a variety of sizes and angles.

CONTINUED ON PAGE 66

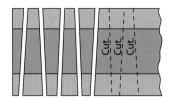

Figure A

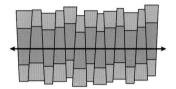

Figure B

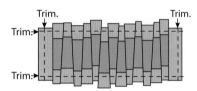

Figure C

Large block

As you cut, keep in mind that ½″ of each wedge will end up as the seam allowance, so each wedge unit should measure at least 1½″ across at its narrowest end. (Figure A)

3. Arrange the wedges into 3 wonky stacks of about 10–14 pieces each, alternating the wide ends of the wedges and the 3 different fabrics. Each wedge should be slightly offset from the wedges on either side of it, but try to keep the edges of the blocks within about 1½″ of one another. (Figure B)

> **tip** Avoid creating a stack that tilts in one direction. It may help to imagine a line running through the middle of the stack. Think about how the wedges are balanced on either side of this line, as though you were making a mobile.

4. Sew the wedges together, adding or removing wedges as necessary to create a pieced stack 19″–21″ tall. Sew 3″ × 10″ pieces of putty solid fabric, centered, to the top and bottom of the stack. Trim the block to 8½″ × 23½″. (Figure C) Repeat to make a total of 3 large grass green blocks.

5. Repeat Steps 1–4 to make 1 large chartreuse block, 1 large avocado block, 2 large coral blocks, and 2 large white blocks.

Large Half-Blocks

1. Arrange and sew 6 or 7 chartreuse wedge units together, as in Large Blocks, Step 3. Sew a 3″ × 10″ piece of putty solid fabric, centered, to one end. Trim this large half-block to 8½″ × 12″.

2. Repeat Step 1 to make 2 large avocado half-blocks, 1 large coral half-block, and 2 large white half-blocks. Set aside the remaining large wedge units for the quilt back.

Large half-block

Medium Blocks

1. Sew a 3″ putty solid fabric strip to each side of each of the 4½″ block fabric strips, creating 15 medium strip sets.

2. Use the same process that was used for the large blocks to cut the strip sets into wedge units. Sew the wedge units together, adding a 3″ × 8″ putty solid piece to each end, to make 4 chartreuse medium blocks and 3 *each* of grass green, avocado, coral, and white medium blocks.

3. Trim the blocks to 6½″ × 23½″. Set aside any remaining medium wedge units for the quilt back.

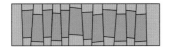

Medium block

Small Blocks

1. Sew a 2½″ putty solid fabric strip to each side of each of the 2½″ block fabric strips, creating 15 small strip sets.

2. Use the same process that you used for the large blocks to cut the strip sets into wedge units. Sew the wedge units together, adding a 3″ × 6″ putty solid piece to each end, to make 4 chartreuse small blocks, 2 grass green small blocks, 4 avocado small blocks, 3 coral small blocks, and 1 white small block.

3. Trim the blocks to 4½″ × 23½″.

Small block

Small Half-Blocks

1. Arrange and sew 6 or 7 grass green wedge units together, sewing a 3″ × 6″ piece of putty solid fabric to one end. Trim this small half-block to 4½″ × 12″.

2. Repeat Step 1 to make 1 small coral half-block and 2 small white half-blocks. Set aside any remaining wedge units for the quilt back.

Small half-block

Making the Quilt Top

Use the quilt top assembly diagram (below) as a guide to arrange the finished blocks and half-blocks in 11 rows. Sew the blocks in each row together. Then join the rows, sewing 2½″ pieces of sashing between the rows and adding a sashing strip to the top and bottom of the quilt top. Press the seams toward the sashing. Trim the sashing even with the sides of the quilt top.

> **tip** I usually press my seams open. However, for quilts like this, I find that when I'm sewing long rows of so many blocks with nonstandard seams, it is more efficient to press the seams to one side.

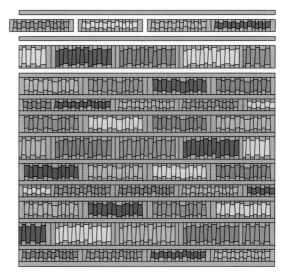
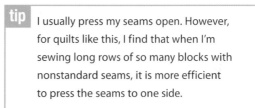

Quilt top assembly diagram

Making the Quilt Back

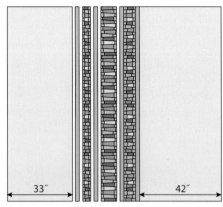

Quilt back assembly diagram

1. Sew the remaining large wedges into 4 stacks, each about 24½″ long, scattering the placement of the different-colored wedges throughout. Sew the 4 stacks together to create a large stack about 96″ long. Square up the sides to 8½″ wide.

2. Repeat Step 1 with the remaining medium wedges, making a 96″ pieced stack 6½″ wide. Repeat again with the remaining small wedges, making a 96″ pieced stack 4½″ wide.

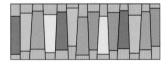

3. Sew together the pieced stacks, the putty solid sashing, and the white solid panels according to the quilt back assembly diagram (above right), pressing the seams toward the putty sashing.

Making the Binding

Sew together the 15 binding pieces (each 2½″ × 25½″) end to end to make a scrappy binding.

Finishing the Quilt

Refer to Construction Basics (pages 132–141) for details on sandwiching, quilting, and binding your project.

Alternate Ideas

make it with favorite prints

It's easy to create fabric trios to highlight a favorite print. In this example, I used monochromatic blue and green prints to coordinate with the blue and green in the multicolor owl print.

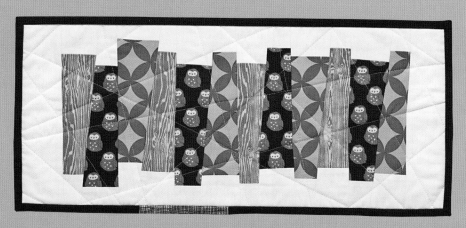

make it sharp

Instead of cutting the strip sets into wedges, cut straight block units of varying widths.

Owl Eyes

Finished block: 12″ × 17″   **Finished quilt:** 54″ × 65¼″   *Made and machine quilted by Elizabeth Hartman*

Appliqué doesn't have to be cute. It can be a great way to use shapes that might be problematic to piece, like these stacked ovals. These shapes remind me of cartoon animal eyes, but they take on a more sophisticated look when organized into blocks.

Selecting the Fabric

This quilt uses a very narrow palette of gray fabrics set off by a single bold color used in a limited way in each quilt block and in a big way on the quilt back. I started with five coordinating gray prints and chose an almost-solid yellow fabric that provides bold contrast. The block backgrounds are made from a gray fabric that's slightly darker than the grays in the prints, and the sashing is the same solid white fabric used in the oval appliqués on the blocks.

Refer to Fabric and Design Vocabulary (page 120) for more about fabric selection.

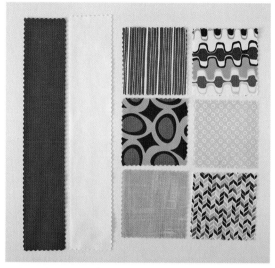

My fabric choices for Owl Eyes

materials

Yardages are based on fabric that is at least 40″ wide, unless otherwise noted.

1 fat quarter (18″ × 21″) *each* of 5 different gray print fabrics for appliqués

4¼ yards yellow almost-solid fabric for appliqués and quilt back

3¼ yards white solid fabric for appliqués and sashing, at least 42″ wide

3 yards gray solid fabric for block backgrounds

⅝ yard binding fabric

58″ × 70″ batting

6¾ yards lightweight paper-backed fusible web, at least 17″ wide

Water-soluble or chalk fabric marker

Translucent template plastic

Pencil

Making the Templates

Use translucent template plastic and the patterns at the back of the book (pullout page P2) to make templates for large oval A, medium oval B, hollow oval C, and small oval D. Refer to Making Templates (page 124) and Cutting Template Shapes (page 129).

cutting instructions

YELLOW SOLID FABRIC:

Cut the fabric into 2 equal-length pieces (about 76″ long).

- From the first piece, cut:

    1 strip 30½″ × length of fabric, for the quilt back

    1 strip 7½″ × length of fabric; subcut into 2 pieces 37½″ × 7½″, for the quilt back

- From the second piece, cut:

    1 strip 16½″ × length of fabric, for the quilt back

- From the remaining fabric, cut:

    1 fat quarter (18″ × 21″)

    2 pieces 7½″ × 16½″

WHITE SOLID FABRIC:

Cut:

- 1 strip 18″ × width of fabric; subcut into 2 fat quarters 21″ × 18″
- 1 strip 12½″ × width of fabric; subcut into 14 sashing strips 2½″ × 12½″
- 4 strips 2½″ × width of fabric; subcut into:

    2 pieces 21½″ × 2½″, for the quilt back

    1 piece 37½″ × 2½″, for the quilt back

    1 piece 16½″ × 2½″, for the quilt back

From the remaining length of fabric (about 79″), cut:

- 3 strips 2½″ × length of fabric; trim to 65¾″ × 2½″
- 1 strip 21″ × length of fabric; subcut the remaining fabric into 4 fat quarters 18″ × 21″

GRAY SOLID FABRIC:

- Cut 8 strips 12½″ × width of fabric; subcut into 15 block bases 17½″ × 12½″

BINDING FABRIC:

- Cut 6 strips 2½″ × width of fabric.

FROM FUSIBLE WEB:

- Cut 12 pieces 17″ × 20″.

Making the Appliqués

1. Following the manufacturer's instructions, iron 17″ × 20″ pieces of fusible web to the wrong side of the 12 fat quarters (6 white solid, 5 gray print, and 1 yellow).

2. Using a pencil, trace 15 large oval A and 15 medium oval B shapes onto the paper backing on each of the 6 white fat quarters. Nestle the shapes close together so they all fit.

3. Trace 15 hollow oval C and 15 small oval D shapes onto the paper backing on each of the 6 remaining fat quarters (5 gray and 1 yellow).

4. Use sharp scissors to cut out all of the appliqué shapes and to remove the centers of the hollow oval C shapes. Sort the shapes by size.

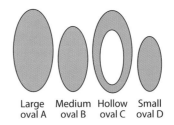

Large   Medium   Hollow   Small
oval A   oval B   oval C   oval D

Making the Blocks

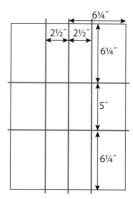

Block placement guide

1. Use a water-soluble or chalk fabric marker and the block placement guide (top right) to mark the placement lines on a 12½″ × 17½″ block base.

 note

> When choosing a fabric marker, always test it on a scrap of the same fabric you're using for your project. Since this project requires pressing the marked areas, pay special attention to whether heat setting will make the marker permanent.

Figure A

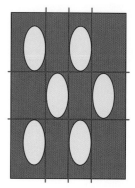

2. Remove the paper backing from the appliqué shapes and position 6 large oval A shapes on the block base placement grid as shown (Figure A). Once you are satisfied with the arrangement, fuse the shapes in place, following the manufacturer's directions.

3. In the remaining 6 spaces, place 5 different gray and 1 yellow hollow oval C shapes. Arrange the shapes so the openings point in alternate directions (up or down) from one column to the next. Carefully place a medium oval B shape under each hollow shape, so the white fabric shows through; fuse in place. (Figure B)

Figure B

4. Place 5 different gray and 1 yellow small oval D shapes on top of each white large oval A shape, positioning each small oval toward one end of a large oval to match the hollow oval C shapes in each column. Fuse in place. (Figure C)

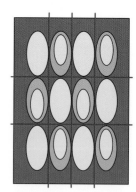

Figure C

5. Repeat Steps 1–4 to make a total of 15 blocks.

6. Use the stitch of your choice to sew around the raw edges of each shape. (See Machine Appliqué Basics, page 131.) I used white thread for the white ovals, yellow thread for the yellow ovals, and gray thread for the gray ovals.

Making the Quilt Top

1. Cut 2 finished blocks in half horizontally, creating 4 half-blocks measuring 12½″ × 8¾″ each. Set aside a block for the quilt back.

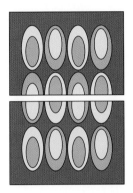

2. Arrange 12 blocks and 4 half-blocks in 4 columns, as shown in the quilt top assembly diagram (top right). Sew together the blocks in each column, with 2½″ × 12½″ pieces of sashing between the blocks. Save the 2 remaining sashing strips for the quilt back.

3. Finish the quilt top by sewing together the 4 columns, with 2½″ × 65¾″ sashing strips between columns.

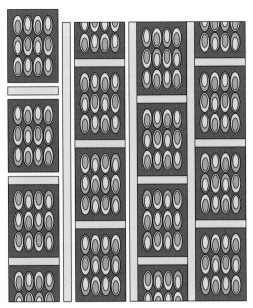

Quilt top assembly diagram

Making the Quilt Back

1. Sew the remaining 2½″ × 12½″ sashing strips to the top and bottom of the remaining block.

2. Sew 2½″ × 21½″ sashing strips to the left and right sides of the block.

3. Sew a 7½″ × 16½″ yellow fabric strip to each side of the 2½″ × 16½″ sashing strip. Sew this pieced unit to the top of the sashed block from Step 2.

4. Sew a 7½″ × 37½″ yellow fabric strip to each side of the 2½″ × 37½″ sashing strip. Sew this pieced unit to the bottom of the sashed block.

5. Finish the quilt back by sewing the 16½″ yellow fabric strip to the *left* side and the 30½″ yellow fabric strip to the *right* side of the pieced back unit.

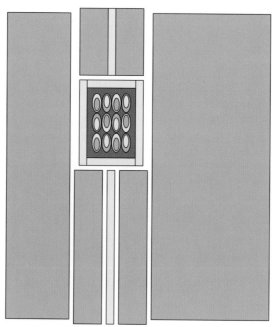

Quilt back assembly diagram

Finishing the Quilt

Refer to Construction Basics (pages 132–141) for details on sandwiching, quilting, and binding your project.

Alternate Ideas

make it scrappy

To make a scrappy version of this quilt, I recommend first tracing the appliqué shapes onto pieces of fusible web and then finding scrap pieces to fit them. To replace the gray and bright-colored pieces for a quilt like this, you'll need 90 of each of the 4 oval shapes.

make it colorful

Replace the pops of gold with a bold print and use coordinating solid fabrics for the rest of the ovals.

Honey

Finished block: 9″ hexagon   **Finished quilt:** 46″ × 63″   *Made and machine quilted by Elizabeth Hartman*

In this quilt design, pyramids become hexagons and hexagons grow into a beautiful honeycomb of bold print and bright solid fabrics.

Selecting the Fabric

The hexagon blocks in this quilt are made with six pairs of fabrics made up of one solid and one contrasting print. I started with six graphic black-and-white prints and chose six bright solids in pinks, reds, and violets to pair with them. The prints all coordinate with one another, as do the bright solids, but the two groups contrast with each other—making the lone print triangle in each hexagon really stand out. To highlight the white in the prints, I chose a light gray for my background fabric.

Refer to Fabric and Design Vocabulary (page 120) for more about fabric selection.

My fabric choices for Honey

materials

Yardages are based on fabric that is at least 40″ wide, unless otherwise noted.

1 yard *each* of 6 different coordinating solid fabrics for blocks

³/₈ yard *each* of 6 different contrasting print fabrics for blocks

4½ yards neutral solid fabric for background (quilt front and back)

½ yard binding fabric

50″ × 67″ batting

Translucent template plastic

Making the Template

Use translucent template plastic and the pattern at the back of the book (pullout page P1) to make the triangle template. Refer to Making Templates (page 124) and Cutting Template Shapes (page 129).

cutting instructions

SOLID FABRICS, FOR BLOCKS:

From *each* of the 6 solid fabrics, cut:

- 4 strips 5½″ × width of fabric
- 2 strips 3½″ × width of fabric

PRINT FABRICS, FOR BLOCKS:

From *each* of the 6 print fabrics, cut:

- 1 strip 5½″ × width of fabric
- 2 strips 1½″ × width of fabric

BACKGROUND FABRIC:

Cut:

- 60 strips 1″ × width of fabric for the block sashing (See Tips at right.)
- 2 strips 5″ × width of fabric for the quilt top background; subcut into:

  1 piece 24″ × 5″

  1 piece 16″ × 5″

  3 strips 10″ × 5″

Use the 60° angle markings on your ruler as a guide to make an angled cut through each of these pieces, as shown in cutting diagram 1 (at right). Label the background pieces A–E, as indicated in the diagram, for the quilt top. Use the triangle template as a guide to square off the pointed ends. (For more information about using the angle markings on your ruler, see Making Angled Cuts, page 129.)

> **tips** Working with Skinny Sashing
>
> - When wrangling skinny sashing, don't try to keep the strips neatly folded. Instead, gently pile them in a plastic bag or bin.
>
> - When cutting strips this skinny, it's especially important to make sure that you're accurately cutting along the grain of the fabric. Off-kilter cuts can result in sashing that warps and doesn't quite line up. Stop every few cuts to make sure that your strips are still coming out straight.
>
> - If you find working with such tiny pieces of sashing problematic, try cutting the sashing ¼″ larger than called for and then trimming it after piecing the half-hexagon units.

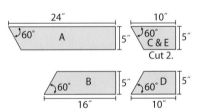

Cutting diagram 1

Trim corner.

CONTINUED ON PAGE 82

Making the Blocks

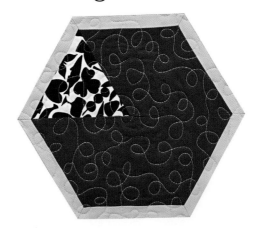

All seam allowances are ¼˝, and all seams are pressed open unless otherwise noted.

- Cut 2 strips 16½˝ × width of fabric.

  Trim away the selvages and use the 60° angle markings on your ruler as a guide to make an angled cut through each of these pieces, as shown in cutting diagram 2 (below). Label the pieces A back, B back, C back, and D back, as indicated in the diagram. Use the triangle template as a guide to square off the pointed ends.

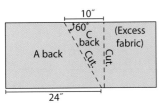

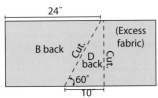

Cutting diagram 2

- From the remaining back-ground fabric (about 59˝), cut 1 strip 14½˝ × *length* of fabric. Label this piece E back; label the remaining fabric F back to be used for the quilt back.

BINDING FABRIC:

- Cut 6 strips 2½˝ × width of fabric.

Block Units

1. Sew a 1˝ sashing strip to each side of each of the 5½˝ print and solid fabric strips, making a total of 30 strip sets.

2. Divide the strip sets into 6 groups, each including 4 of the same color solid and 1 print. Assign each group a number, 1 through 6.

3. Use the triangle template to cut triangular block units from the strip sets. Keep the bottom of the template lined up with the outside edge of the sashing fabric, and alternate sides to get as many triangles as you can from each strip set. The block unit cutting guide (below) tells you how many units to cut from the strip sets in each of the 6 groups.

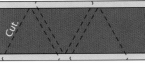

Cutting block units

	Solid units	Print units
1	35	7
2	31	8
3	32	8
4	36	8
5	32	8
6	35	7

Block unit cutting guide

Half-Hexagons

Each half-hexagon is made up of three triangular block units. To sew the units together accurately, match both the seams where the sashing and block fabrics meet and the squared-off tops of the triangles. On a perfectly pieced half-hexagon, the sashing will line up, and the point where the three triangles meet will be ¼˝ from the top.

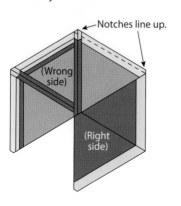

Making half-hexagons

Using the quilt top assembly diagram (at right) as a guide and working one row at a time, sew the block units into half-hexagons. Note that the partial hexagons at the ends of most rows will be made with just two block units.

Making the Quilt Top

1. Still following the quilt top assembly diagram and working a row at a time, sew the half-hexagon units into 14 rows. Rows 1 through 5 will also include background pieces A, B, C, D, and E. Use the squared-off points of the triangle units to accurately line up the half-hexagons before you sew.

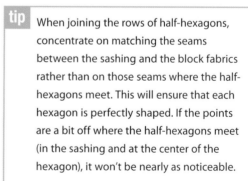

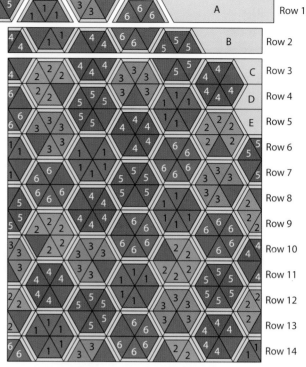

Quilt top assembly diagram

2. Sew the 14 rows together and square off the sides of the finished quilt top to create a rectangle approximately 46½˝ × 63½˝.

> **tip** When joining the rows of half-hexagons, concentrate on matching the seams between the sashing and the block fabrics rather than on those seams where the half-hexagons meet. This will ensure that each hexagon is perfectly shaped. If the points are a bit off where the half-hexagons meet (in the sashing and at the center of the hexagon), it won't be nearly as noticeable.

Making the Quilt Back

1. Sew each print strip 1½″ × width of fabric to a corresponding solid strip 3½″ × width of fabric, matching the long sides. Make a total of 12 strip sets.

2. Pair like-colored solid strip sets and cut 1 unit each 22″, 16″, 12″, and 8″ long from each paired set.

3. Divide the cut units into 6 groups, with each group including a unit in each of the 4 sizes.

4. Sew the units in each group together, in order of size, with the longest on the bottom and subsequent layers centered on top of it like a wedding cake. The bottom layer of each 16½″-tall "cake" should be a print fabric, and the top layer should be a solid.

5. Use the triangle template as a guide, as shown, to cut the 6 cakes into 6 triangular block units 16½″ tall. Use the template to square off all the points of each triangle.

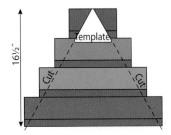

6. Sew the 6 triangular block units into 2 half-hexagon units, matching the seams between the print and solid fabric strips.

7. Sew the back pieces together as shown on the quilt back assembly diagram. When sewing together angled pieces, line them up the same way you did for the quilt top.

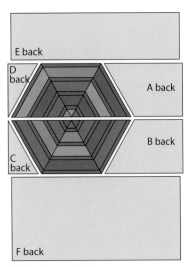

Quilt back assembly diagram

Finishing the Quilt

Refer to Construction Basics (pages 132–141) for details on sandwiching, quilting, and binding your project.

Alternate Ideas

make it bold

Instead of using a white or light background fabric, try something more dramatic. The dark chocolate brown that I used here really makes the aquamarines and oranges pop.

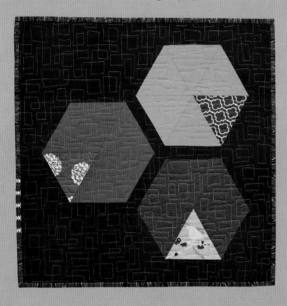

make it scrappy

Of course, you don't have to stick with the 5 parts solid, 1 part print formula that I used. Making all 6 segments in each hexagon different can produce a wonderfully scrappy look. Just substitute 30 assorted strips 5½″ × width of fabric for the ones called for in the pattern. Use the strip sets to cut a total of 247 triangular block units. For the giant hexagon block on the quilt back, substitute 6 strips each in the following sizes:

3½″ × 22″	1½″ × 22″
3½″ × 16″	1½″ × 16″
3½″ × 12″	1½″ × 12″
3½″ × 8″	1½″ × 8″

Looptastic

Finished block: 21″ × 21″   **Finished quilt:** 84″ × 84″   *Made and machine quilted by Elizabeth Hartman*

What could be more fun than giant patchwork loops? Giant patchwork loops made with a shortcut sew-and-turn appliqué method, that's what. It's *Looptastic!*

Selecting the Fabric

The loops in this project are made with three sets of coordinating fabrics in teal, chartreuse, and white, with each set including one solid and three prints. The intense colors and bright white stand out against a dull gray solid background fabric. The solid fabric in each color group is also used for large panels on the quilt back and for the binding.

If you look at my fabric choices, you can see that the fabrics for the white rings actually include an awful lot of teal. I didn't want to have a bunch of all-white fabrics in these loops, so I chose prints that featured white in a prominent way and used teal as a secondary color. Because the teal group is darker and more intense, the white group still stands out.

Refer to Fabric and Design Vocabulary (page 120) for more about fabric selection.

My fabric choices for Looptastic

materials

Yardages are based on fabric that is at least 40˝ wide, unless otherwise noted.

7 yards light gray solid fabric for background

3⅝ yards chartreuse solid fabric, at least 42˝ wide

1 yard *each* of 3 different chartreuse print fabrics

3½ yards teal solid fabric, at least 42˝ wide

⅞ yard *each* of 3 different teal print fabrics

¾ yard *each* of 3 different white prints and 1 white solid fabric

¾ yard binding fabric

88˝ × 88˝ batting

Translucent template plastic

9 plastic sandwich bags

16 yards lightweight sew-in interfacing, 22˝ wide

> **tip** Sew-in interfacing usually comes in white or black. Choose the color that best matches your background fabric. Fusible interfacing isn't recommended, because you sew the appliqué units together (and press the seams open) before you attach the loops to the quilt block backgrounds. Sew-in interfacing is much easier to work with under these conditions.

Making the Templates

Use translucent template plastic and the patterns at the back of the book (pullout page P2) to make templates for A1, A2, A3, B1, B2, B3, C1, C2, and C3. Refer to Making Templates (page 124) and Cutting Template Shapes (page 129).

cutting instructions

This quilt uses many different pieces, cut from lots of different fabrics. Use labeled sandwich bags to keep them in order while you work. Label the 9 bags as follows: A1, A2, A3, B1, B2, B3, C1, C2, and C3. Sort the pieces into the appropriate bags as you cut the template pieces.

LIGHT GRAY BACKGROUND FABRIC:

Cut:

- 11 strips 21½″ × width of fabric

   From 8 of the strips, subcut each into:

   1 block base 21½″ × 21½″ and
   1 half-block base 11″ × 21½″

   From the remaining 3 strips, subcut each into:

   1 block base 21½″ × 21½″ and
   1 quarter-block base 11″ × 11″

- 1 strip 11″ × width of fabric; subcut into 1 quarter-block base 11″ × 11″

You should now have a total of 11 block bases, 8 half-block bases, and 4 quarter-block bases.

CHARTREUSE SOLID FABRIC:

Cut:

- 1 strip 5″ × width of fabric; subcut into 5 circles using Template B1

- 2 strips 4½″ × width of fabric; subcut into 20 wedge shapes using Template C2

- 3 strips 4″ × width of fabric; subcut into 24 wedge shapes using Template A3

- 1 strip 4½″ × width of fabric for the quilt back

- From the remaining fabric, trim to 92½″ for the quilt back; subcut into:

   1 strip 18½″ × 92½″

   1 strip 22½″ × 92½″

CHARTREUSE PRINT FABRIC:

From *each* chartreuse print fabric, cut:

- 3 strips 4½″ × width of fabric; subcut into 20 wedge shapes using Template C2

- 3 strips 4″ × width of fabric; subcut into 24 wedge shapes using Template A3

- 1 strip 4½″ × width of fabric for the quilt back

TEAL SOLID FABRIC:

Cut:

- 1 strip 6″ × width of fabric; subcut into 5 circles using Template C1

- 3 strips 4¾″ × width of fabric; subcut into 20 wedge shapes using Template B3

- 2 strips 3½″ × width of fabric; subcut into 24 wedge shapes using Template A2

- 1 strip 4½″ × width of fabric for the quilt back

- From the remaining fabric, trim to 92½″ for the quilt back; subcut into:

   1 strip 18½″ × 92½″

   1 strip 22½″ × 92½″

CONTINUED ON PAGE 90

TEAL PRINT FABRIC:

From *each* teal print fabric, cut:

- 3 strips 4¾″ × width of fabric; subcut into 20 wedge shapes using Template B3

- 2 strips 3½″ × width of fabric; subcut into 24 wedge shapes using Template A2

- 1 strip 4½″ × width of fabric for the quilt back

WHITE PRINT AND SOLID FABRIC:

From *each* of the 3 white prints and 1 white solid fabric, cut:

- 2 strips 2¼″ × width of fabric; subcut into 24 wedge shapes using Template A1

- 3 strips 3″ × width of fabric; subcut into 40 wedge shapes using Template C3

- 1 strip 4½″ × width of fabric; subcut into 10 wedge shapes using Template B2

- 1 strip 4½″ × width of fabric for the quilt back

INTERFACING:

Cut 32 pieces 18″ × width of interfacing (22″).

BINDING FABRIC:

Cut 9 strips 2½″ × width of fabric.

Making the Blocks

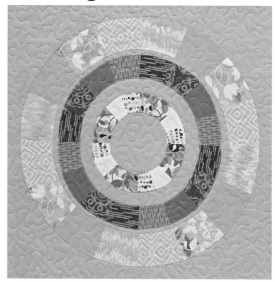

All seam allowances are ¼″, and all seams are pressed open unless otherwise noted.

Block A

Pieced Units

1. Sew sets of 4 different A1 wedge shapes together, pressing the seams open, to make 24 quarter-loop units. Then sew together sets of 2 quarter-loop units to make 12 half-loop units.

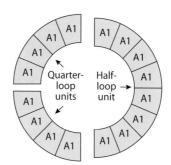

2. Repeat Step 1 to make 12 half-loop units from the A2 wedge shapes and 12 from the A3 wedge shapes. You should have 12 half-loops in each of the 3 sizes.

Loops

1. Place 1 half-loop of each size (A1, A2, and A3) facedown on an 18″ × 22″ piece of lightweight sew-in interfacing, nesting them slightly to fit. Pin them in place and trim the interfacing to within about ¼″ of the unit edges.

2. Sew around both curved edges of each pieced unit, using a ¼″ seam allowance and leaving both ends open. Trim the interfacing even with the fabric and save the interfacing scraps for making the centers of Blocks B and C.

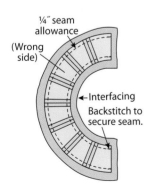

¼″ seam allowance

(Wrong side)

Interfacing
Backstitch to secure seam.

3. Clip the inner curves and carefully turn the half-loops right side out through the short open ends, using a chopstick or another blunt object as necessary to help turn them. Press flat. You should now have 12 finished half-loops in each of the 3 sizes.

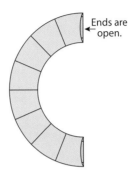

Ends are open.

4. Place 2 identical half-loop units on a cutting mat, right sides together. Make sure the 2 halves are lined up perfectly; use a rotary cutter and ruler to carefully square up the raw edges.

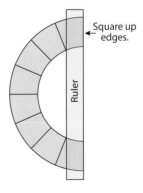

Square up edges.

Ruler

5. Sew the 2 identical half-loops together to create a full loop. Press the seams open and trim away any excess interfacing. Repeat with 10 of the remaining half-loops to create 5 full loops in each size. (There will be 2 remaining half-loops in each size for use later.)

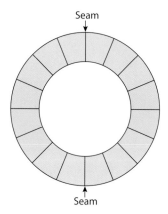

Attaching the Loops

1. Place a block base on a cutting mat and fold it in half, finger-pressing a crease down the center. Unfold the fabric and refold in the opposite direction, finger-pressing again to make another crease down the center, perpendicular to the first.

2. Using the creases as a guide, center one of the smallest loops on the block base and pin it securely in place.

3. Use the stitch of your choice to attach the loop to the base, sewing the inner curve first and then the outer curve. (See Machine Appliqué Basics, page 131, for more information.)

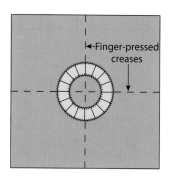

> **tip** I prefer the ease of using my sewing machine, but you can certainly hand appliqué the loops if you prefer.

4. Use the same method from Step 3 to add 1 each of the 2 subsequent-sized loops, one at a time, always stitching around the innermost curve first and working your way out.

Repeat Steps 1–4 to make a total of 5 Block A units.

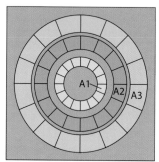

Block A—Make 5.

5. Place a half-block base on your cutting mat and fold it in half, matching 11˝ sides and finger-pressing a crease down the middle. Using the crease as a guide, center one of the smallest half-loops on the half-block base, lining up the raw edges. Pin and sew the half-loop in place.

6. Following the same method you used with the full blocks, add subsequent-sized half-loops to make 2 Half-Block A units.

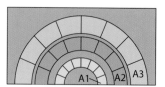

Half-Block A—Make 2.

Block B

Center Circles

1. Place a B1 circle facedown on a scrap of interfacing that is slightly larger than the circle; pin in place. Sew the circle to the interfacing using a ¼″ seam allowance; then trim the interfacing to match the edge of the fabric circle.

2. With scissors, cut a slit in the center of the interfacing. Use this opening to turn the circle right side out, pushing out the edges with a chopstick or other blunt tool. Press the circle flat.

3. Repeat Steps 1 and 2 to make a total of 5 circles.

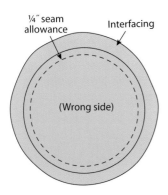

Pieced Units

1. Sew sets of 2 different B2 wedge shapes together, pressing the seams open, to make 20 quarter-loop units. Then sew sets of 2 quarter-loop units together to make 9 half-loop units. There will be 2 remaining quarter-loops for use later.

2. Sew sets of 4 different B3 wedge shapes together, pressing the seams open, to make 20 quarter-loop units. Then sew sets of 2 quarter-loop units together to make 9 half-loop units. There will be 2 remaining quarter-loops for use later.

Loops

1. Following the directions for Block A loops (page 91), make 9 interface-finished B2 and B3 half-loops in each size.

2. Join identical paired B2 and B3 half-loops together to make 3 finished full loops in each size. (There will be 3 remaining finished half-loops in each size for use later.)

3. Finish the remaining 2 quarter-loops in each size (B2 and B3), attaching the interfacing, clipping the curves, and turning the pieces right side out, following the directions for Block A loops (page 91).

Attaching the Loops

1. Use the same method as for Block A to attach the loops (page 92) finger-pressing the creases into a block base and centering a finished B1 circle on the base. Pin and sew in place.

2. Add 1 each of the 2 subsequent-sized loops (B2, B3) to the block base, one at a time. Stitch around the innermost curve first and work your way out.

3. Repeat Steps 1 and 2 to create 3 full-loop Block B units.

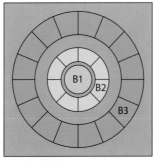

Block B—Make 3.

4. Cut the remaining finished B1 circles in half. Place a half-block base on your cutting mat and fold it in half, matching the 11″ sides and finger-pressing a crease down the middle. Using the crease as a guide, center a half-circle on the half-block base, lining up the raw edges. Pin and sew the half-circle in place.

5. Use the remaining half-loops to make 3 Half-Block B units, sewing 1 each of the B2 and B3 subsequent-sized half-loops to the half block base, one at a time.

6. Repeat Steps 4 and 5 to make a total of 3 Half-Block B units.

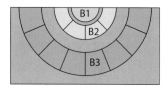

Half-Block B—Make 3.

7. Cut the remaining half-circle in half, creating 2 equal quarters. Use these and the remaining finished quarter-loops to make 2 Quarter-Block B units.

Quarter-Block B—Make 2.

Block C

Center Circles

Use the C1 fabric circles and the same method used for Block B center circles (page 93) and leftover interfacing to make 5 finished C1 circles.

Pieced Units

1. Sew sets of 4 different C2 wedge shapes together, pressing the seams open, to make 20 quarter-loop units. Then sew sets of 2 quarter-loop units together to make 9 half-loop units. There will be 2 remaining quarter-loops for use later.

2. Sew sets of 8 different C3 wedge shapes together, pressing the seams open, to make 20 quarter-loop units. Then sew sets of 2 quarter-loop units together to make 9 half-loop units. There will be 2 remaining quarter-loops for use later.

Loops

1. Use the same process as for Block A (page 91) to make 9 finished C2 and C3 half-loops in each size.

2. Join identical paired C2 and C3 half-loops together to make 3 finished full loops in each size. There will be 3 remaining half-loops in each size for use later.

3. Finish the remaining 2 quarter-loops in each size (C2 and C3), attaching the interfacing, clipping the curves, and turning the pieces right side out, following the directions for Block A loops (page 91).

Attaching the Loops

1. Use the same method as for Block B to attach the loops (page 93) but use the C1, C2, and C3 units to make 3 Block C units.

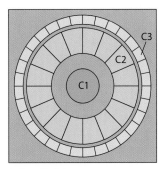

Make 3. Block C

2. Use the instructions from Block B (pages 93 and 94) and the remaining C1, C2, and C3 units to make 3 Half-Block C units and 2 Quarter-Block C units.

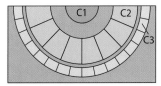

Half-Block C—Make 3.

Quarter-Block C—Make 2.

Finishing the Quilt Top

Sew the blocks, half-blocks, and quarter-blocks into 5 rows as shown in the quilt top assembly diagram. Sew together the 5 rows to complete the quilt top.

Quilt top assembly diagram

Making the Quilt Back

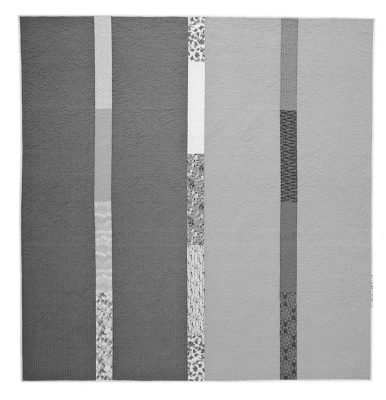

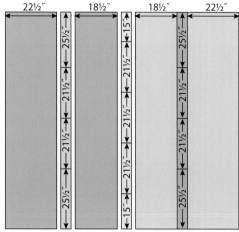

Quilt back assembly diagram

Finishing the Quilt

Refer to Construction Basics (pages 132–141) for details on sandwiching, quilting, and binding your project.

1. Trim 2 of the 4½″ chartreuse print strips to measure 25½″. Trim the other 4½″ chartreuse print strip and the 4½″ chartreuse solid strip to measure 21½″. Sew the pieces end to end, beginning and ending with a 25½″ piece.

2. Repeat Step 1 using the 4½″ teal print and solid strips.

3. Cut a 4½″ white print strip into 2 pieces 4½″ × 15″. Trim the other 2 white 4½″ print strips and the white 4½″ solid piece to measure 21½″. Sew these pieces end to end, beginning and ending with a 15″ piece.

4. Sew the pieced strips and solid back pieces together in the following order, matching the long sides: 22½″ teal solid, 4½″ chartreuse strip, 18½″ teal solid, 4½″ white strip, 18½″ chartreuse solid, 4½″ teal strip, and 22½″ chartreuse solid.

Alternate Ideas

make it scrappy

Instead of cutting from new yardage, cut the template pieces from scraps. Separate the 9 different shapes into plastic sandwich bags to keep everything organized. You'll need:

96 pieces each of A1, A2, and A3

5 pieces of B1

40 pieces of B2

80 pieces of B3

5 pieces of C1

80 pieces of C2

160 pieces of C3

In this example, I used all solid fabrics and arranged my scraps in color-wheel order.

make it with coordinates

Making all the loops and circles in the same basic colors can be a great opportunity to high-light a collection of coordinating print fabrics.

Happy Hour

Finished block: 8″ × 16″   **Finished quilt:** 48″ × 56″   *Made and machine quilted by Elizabeth Hartman*

The blocks in this quilt are similar in concept to the traditional Drunkard's Path pattern. I've just stretched the block to create a longer capsule shape instead of a circle. The elongated shape reminds me of cinder blocks, so I staggered the blocks and varied the background solids to resemble masonry. On the quilt back, which is arranged a bit differently, the blocks create a dramatic secondary pattern.

Sewing curves like these takes a little maneuvering, but it's totally doable. Take your time and don't hesitate to remove seams and start over until you get it right.

Selecting the Fabric

The simple shapes in this pattern are perfect for showing off exciting prints, so I started with seven bold multicolor ones. I then chose seven solid fabrics in bright jewel tones to match the prints and a light gray solid for my neutral background.

Refer to Fabric and Design Vocabulary (page 120) for more about fabric selection.

My fabric choices for **Happy Hour**

materials

Yardages are based on fabric that is at least 40˝ wide, unless otherwise noted.

½ yard *each* of 7 different print fabrics

¼ yard *each* of 7 coordinating bright solid fabrics

4½ yards neutral background solid fabric

½ yard binding fabric

52˝ × 60˝ batting

Translucent template plastic

Making the Templates

Use translucent template plastic and the patterns at the back of the book (pullout page P1) to make templates for A and B. Refer to Making Templates (page 124) and Cutting Template Shapes (page 129).

cutting instructions

The capsule shapes at the centers of the blocks are created with pieces cut in the template shapes and pieces cut in the mirror image of those shapes. The cutting instructions tell you which pieces should be cut with the templates facing right side up (up) and which pieces should be cut in mirror image, with the templates facing down (down).

PRINT FABRICS:

From *each* print fabric, cut:

- 2 strips 4½″ × width of fabric; subcut into 8 Template B pieces, 4 up and 4 down
- 2 strips 2½″ × width of fabric; subcut into 8 Template A pieces, 4 up and 4 down

BRIGHT SOLID FABRICS:

From *each* bright solid fabric, cut:

- 1 strip 4½″ × width of fabric; subcut into 4 Template B pieces, 2 up and 2 down

BACKGROUND FABRIC:

Cut:

- 14 strips 4½″ × width of fabric; subcut into 56 Template B pieces, 28 up and 28 down
- 14 strips 2½″ × width of fabric; subcut into 84 Template A pieces, 42 up and 42 down

- Trim the remaining background fabric to measure 56½″ for the quilt back; subcut into:

  1 piece 12½″ × 56½″

  1 piece 20½″ × 56½″

BINDING FABRIC:

- Cut 6 strips 2½″ × width of fabric.

Making the Blocks

Print Blocks

1. Start with 1 print piece B and 1 background solid piece A. With right sides together, match the marks at the center of the curves and pin in place.

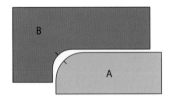

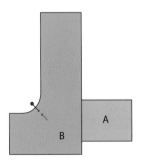

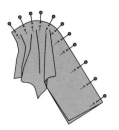

Figure A

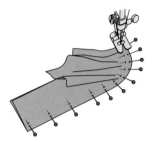

Figure B

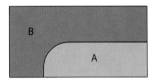

Figure C

Figure D
Down block component   **Figure E**
Up block component

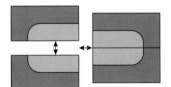

Figure F

2. Match and pin the ends of the pieces together, with piece B on top. Continue adding pins, easing the curves so all the raw edges align and the pieces are secured with pins. (Figure A)

3. Keeping piece B on top, carefully sew around the curve, using a ¼″ seam allowance and removing the pins as you go. The concave piece won't lie flat, but that's fine. Just remember to turn the pieces ever so slightly as you go and try to avoid inadvertently sewing in pleats. Stop and readjust midcurve as necessary. (Figure B)

4. Make a few ⅛″ clips around the curve and press the seam toward piece A.

> **tips**
>
> • If you normally use a ¼″ patchwork foot with an attached guide on your sewing machine, you may want to switch back to a standard foot while piecing the curved seams on these blocks. With so much going on in a small space, having that extra little piece of metal out of the way can be helpful.
>
> • When working with other bias-cut pieces, such as triangles and diamonds, we typically try to avoid stretching or warping the edges. However, when piecing curves, being able to manipulate the bias-cut edges is actually a huge help. Feel free to pull and prod to get the curve just right.

5. Square up the curved unit to 4½″ × 8½″. (Figure C)

6. Repeat Steps 1–5 with the same fabric to make a total of 2 identical and 2 mirror-image units (2 up and 2 down). (Figures D and E)

7. Sew each pair of mirror-image units together, matching the seams, to create a half-block that has a "U" shape. Sew the 2 halves together to complete the block. (Figure F)

Print block

8. Repeat Steps 1–7 to make 1 block from each print fabric (7 blocks total).

Bright Blocks

Repeat Print Blocks, Steps 1–7 (pages 100–102), to sew 28 bright solid B pieces and 28 background solid A pieces into 7 bright blocks.

Bright block

> **tip** Although it's easy to identify the mirror-image pieces of the print fabrics, the pieces you cut from the bright solid fabrics may be nearly impossible to tell apart, because the color may be the same on both sides of the fabric. If you can't tell the difference, don't worry about trying to keep track of the right and wrong side of every cut piece. Just make sure that you're sewing an equal number of mirror-image units from each fabric.

Background Solid Blocks

1. Repeat Print Blocks, Steps 1–7 (pages 100–102), to sew 28 background solid B pieces and 28 print A pieces into 28 curved units (14 up and 14 down).

2. Sew 4 sets of matching units to make 4 background blocks.

3. Sew the remaining curved units into 3 pairs of identical half-blocks (6 total half-blocks). Set aside the remaining A and B units for the quilt back.

Background block

Half-block

Making the Quilt Top

Follow the quilt top assembly diagram to arrange the finished blocks and half-blocks in 7 rows. Sew the blocks in each row together; then sew the rows together to finish the quilt top.

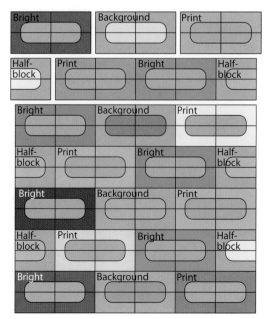

Quilt top assembly diagram

Making the Quilt Back

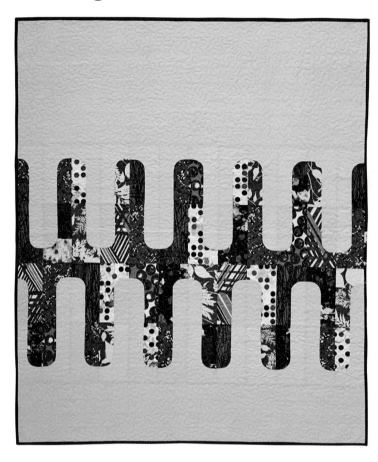

3. Arrange the units in 4 rows of 14 according to the quilt back assembly diagram; sew each row together. Sew the rows and the solid quilt back panels together as indicated to finish the quilt back.

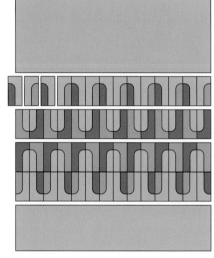

Quilt back assembly diagram

1. Use the 28 remaining print B pieces and the 28 remaining background solid A pieces to make 28 curved units, 14 up and 14 down.

2. Use the 28 remaining background solid B pieces and the 28 remaining print A pieces to make 28 more curved units, 14 up and 14 down.

Up   Down   Up   Down

Block units for quilt back

Finishing the Quilt

Refer to Construction Basics (pages 132–141) for details on sandwiching, quilting, and binding your project.

Alternate Ideas

make it scrappy

Make the block units from a variety of fabric scraps. To substitute scraps for the print and solid yardage called for in the pattern, you'll need 56 pieces cut from Template A and 84 scrap pieces cut from Template B.

make it with solids

The simple graphic shape of this block is a wonderful complement to bold-colored solid fabrics.

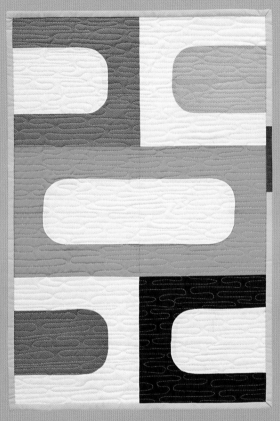

Escape Artist

Finished block: 21″ × 21″   **Finished quilt:** 68″ × 68″   *Made and machine quilted by Elizabeth Hartman*

The graphic, gridded blocks on this quilt are reminiscent of a woven paper placemat, or part of a screen door. The blocks are made with strip-pieced units, which offer a great chance to practice your precision piecing skills. The quilt top includes one "opposite" block, and the quilt back features a surprising giant version of the same block.

Selecting the Fabric

This quilt is made almost entirely from three solid fabrics: a light neutral, a dark neutral, and a bright solid fabric. They can all be variations of the same color, but there should be enough contrast among them that the gridded piecing shows up clearly. For my quilt, I chose white for the light negative space, charcoal gray for the dark grids, and vibrant turquoise for the opposite block and quilt back. I highlighted each block with a skinny strip of turquoise or gray print fabric.

Refer to Fabric and Design Vocabulary (page 120) for more about fabric selection.

My fabric choices for Escape Artist

materials

Yardages are based on fabric that is at least 40˝ wide, unless otherwise noted.

5½ yards light neutral solid fabric for background

1⅝ yards dark solid fabric for grids

5½ yards bright solid fabric for quilt back and opposite block

12 print fabric scraps, at least 2˝ × 16˝, for accent grids

⅓ yard print fabric for quilt back accent grid

⅝ yard binding

72˝ × 72˝ batting

cutting instructions

LIGHT NEUTRAL SOLID FABRIC:

For the contrasting block, cut:

- 1 strip 7″ × width of fabric; subcut into:

  1 piece 5½″ × 7″

  1 piece 4½″ × 7″

  1 piece 3½″ × 7″

  1 piece 2½″ × 7″

  6 pieces 1½″ × 7″

  From the remaining fabric, cut 4 pieces 1½″ × 9½″.

For the main blocks, cut:

- 11 strips 6½″ × width of fabric; subcut into:

  32 corner squares 6½″ × 6½″

  128 spacer strips 1½″ × 6½″

- 1 strip 5½″ × width of fabric

- 2 strips 4½″ × width of fabric

- 2 strips 3½″ × width of fabric

- 2 strips 2½″ × width of fabric

- 9 strips 1½″ × width of fabric; subcut 2 of these strips into:

  9 pieces 1½″ × 1½″

  7 pieces 5½″ × 1½″

For the back block, cut:

- 2 strips 15″ × width of fabric; subcut into:

  1 piece 15½″ × 15″

  1 piece 12½″ × 15″

  1 piece 9½″ × 15″

  1 piece 6½″ × 15″

  6 pieces 3½″ × 15″

- 4 strips 3½″ × width of fabric; subcut into 4 grid strips 27½″ × 3½″

For the sashing, cut:

- 6 strips 2½″ × width of fabric; subcut *each* strip into:

  1 medium sashing strip 21½″ × 2½″ (6 total)

  1 short sashing strip 10½″ × 2½″ (6 total)

- 6 more strips 2½″ × width of fabric; sew in sets of 2 along the short ends; and then trim to make 3 long sashing strips each 68½″ × 2½″

DARK SOLID FABRIC:

For the grids, cut:

- 1 strip 9½″ × width of fabric; subcut into 18 pieces 1½″ × 9½″

- 1 strip 4½″ × width of fabric; subcut into 22 pieces 1½″ × 4½″

- 1 strip 5½″ × width of fabric

- 2 strips 4½″ × width of fabric

- 2 strips 3½″ × width of fabric

- 2 strips 2½″ × width of fabric

- 8 strips 1½″ × width of fabric

BRIGHT SOLID FABRIC:

For the contrasting block, cut:

- 1 strip 7″ × width of fabric; subcut into:

  1 piece 5½″ × 7″

  1 piece 4½″ × 7″

  1 piece 3½″ × 7″

  1 piece 2½″ × 7″

  5 pieces 1½″ × 7″

- 2 strips 6½″ × width of fabric; subcut into:

  4 corner squares 6½″ × 6½″

  1 piece 1½″ × 1½″

  1 piece 1½″ × 5½″

  16 spacer strips 1½″ × 6½″

CONTINUED ON PAGE 110

For the back block, cut:

- 1 strip 3½″ × width of fabric; subcut into:

  1 piece 3½″ × 3½″

  1 piece 9½″ × 3½″

- 2 strips 15″ × width of fabric; subcut into:

  1 piece 15½″ × 15″

  1 piece 12½″ × 15″

  1 piece 9½″ × 15″

  1 piece 6½″ × 15″

  6 pieces 3½″ × 15″

- 4 strips 18½″ × width of fabric; subcut into:

  4 corner squares 18½″ × 18½″

  16 spacer strips 3½″ × 18½″

  From the remaining length of the fabric, cut:

  2 border strips 7″ × 63½″

  2 border strips 7″ × 76½″

PRINT SCRAPS:

For the accent grids, cut:

- 6 pieces 1½″ × 15½″ (1 of these pieces is for the contrast block)

- 2 pieces 1½″ × 5½″

- 4 pieces 1½″ × 9½″

PRINT FABRIC:

For the quilt back block accent grid, cut 2 strips 3½″ × width of fabric.

BINDING FABRIC:

Cut 8 strips 2½″ × width of fabric.

Making the Block Units

Refer to the pieced block units illustration (next page).

1. Sew a light solid 1½″ × width of fabric strip to the top of a 5½″ dark solid strip, matching the long sides. Subcut the strip set into 17 pieced A units measuring 1½″ × 6½″.

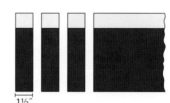

1½″

2. Repeat with 2 light strips 2½″ × width of fabric and 2 dark 4½″ solid strips, subcutting the 2 strip sets to create a total of 32 pieced B units 1½″ × 6½″.

3. Repeat with 2 light and 2 dark strips 3½˝ × width of fabric, subcutting the 2 strip sets to create a total of 32 pieced C units 1½˝ × 6½˝.

4. Repeat with 2 light strips 4½˝ × width of fabric and 2 dark 2½˝ strips, subcutting the strip sets to create 32 pieced D units 1½˝ × 6½˝.

5. Repeat with a light strip 5½˝ × width of fabric and a 1½˝ dark strip, subcutting to create 19 pieced E units 1½˝ × 6½˝.

6. Sew together 5 dark and 4 light strips 1½˝ × width of fabric, matching the long sides; alternate fabrics, beginning and ending with a dark strip. Subcut into 20 pieced F units 1½˝ × 9½˝.

7. Sew together 2 dark and 2 light strips 1½˝ × width of fabric, alternating fabrics. Subcut into 24 pieced G units 1½˝ × 4½˝.

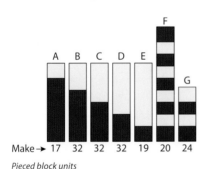

Make → 17 32 32 32 19 20 24

Pieced block units

Making Blocks 6, 10, and 11

When sewing together block units and spacer units, the dark part of the block unit should always be on the bottom.

Refer to the labeled parts of the assembly diagram for Blocks 6, 10, and 11 (page 112).

1. Sew together 1 unit D, 1 unit B, 1 unit E, and 3 light spacer strips 1½˝ × 6½˝. Alternate the block units with the spacer strips, starting with a block unit and ending with a spacer strip.

2. Sew a 1½˝ × 6½˝ spacer strip to the left side of a unit C.

3. Sew together 1 each of units C, E, A, D, and B, sewing 1½˝ × 6½˝ spacer strips between adjoining block units.

4. Sew together 3 dark grid strips 1½˝ × 9½˝ and 3 unit F pieces, beginning with a grid strip and alternating the pieces.

5. Sew a 1½˝ × 1½˝ light square to the top of a 1½˝ × 15½˝ print scrap accent grid strip. Sew a 1½˝ × 5½˝ light strip to the bottom of the print scrap strip.

6. Sew a 1½˝ × 9½˝ dark grid strip to the right side of a unit F.

7. Sew together 1 each of units D, B, E, A, and C, sewing 1½˝ × 6½˝ spacer strips between adjoining block units.

8. Sew together 3 spacer strips and 1 each of units A, D, and B, starting with a 1½˝ × 6½˝ spacer strip and alternating the pieces.

9. Sew a 1½˝ × 6½˝ spacer strip to the right side of a unit C.

10. Sew together the 9 pieced units and 4 corner squares 6½″ × 6½″ to make a finished block.

11. Repeat Steps 1–10 to make a total of 3 identical blocks (Blocks 6, 10, and 11).

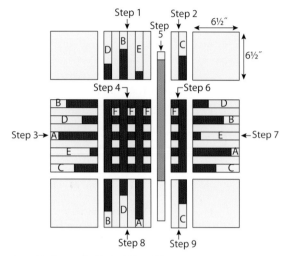

Assembly diagram for Blocks 6, 10, and 11

Finished Blocks 6, 10, and 11

Making Half-Blocks 2 and 15

Refer to the labeled parts of the assembly diagram for Half-Blocks 2 and 15 (at right).

1. Sew together 1 each of units D, B, and E with 3 spacer 1½″ × 6½″ strips, alternating block units and spacer strips and starting with a block unit.

2. Sew a 1½″ × 6½″ spacer strip to the left side of a unit C.

3. Sew together 2 spacer 1½″ × 6½″ strips, 1 unit D, and 1 unit B, alternating spacer strips and block units and starting with a spacer strip.

4. Sew together 3 unit G pieces and 3 dark grid strips 1½″ × 4½″, alternating grid strips and block units and starting with a block unit.

5. Sew a 1½″ light fabric square to the top of a 1½″ × 9½″ print scrap accent grid strip.

6. Sew a 1½″ × 4½″ dark grid strip to the left side of a unit G.

7. Sew together 1 unit D, 1 unit B, and 2 spacer 1½″ × 6½″ strips, alternating block units and spacer strips and beginning with unit D.

8. Sew together the 7 pieced units and 2 corner squares 6½″ × 6½″ to make a finished half-block.

9. Repeat Steps 1–8 to make a total of 2 identical half-blocks (Blocks 2 and 15).

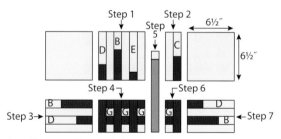

Assembly diagram for Half-Blocks 2 and 15

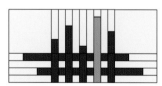

Finished Half-Blocks 2 and 15

Making Half-Blocks 3 and 14

Refer to the labeled parts of the assembly diagram for Half-Blocks 3 and 14 (below).

1. Sew together 2 spacer 1½″ × 6½″ strips, 1 unit D, and 1 unit B, alternating spacer strips and block units and beginning with a spacer strip.

2. Sew together 2 unit F and 2 dark grid strips 1½″ × 9½″, alternating block units and grid strips and starting with a block unit.

3. Sew together 1 each of units C, E, A, D, and B and 4 spacer 1½″ × 6½″ strips, alternating block units and spacer strips and beginning and ending with a block unit.

4. Sew together 1 unit D, 1 unit B, and 2 spacer 1½″ × 6½″ strips, alternating block units and spacer strips and beginning with a block unit.

5. Sew together the 4 pieced units and 2 corner squares 6½″ × 6½″ to make a finished half-block.

6. Repeat Steps 1–5 to make a total of 2 identical half-blocks (Blocks 3 and 14).

Making Half-Blocks 5 and 12

Refer to the labeled parts of the assembly diagram for Half-Blocks 5 and 12 (below).

1. Sew together 1 each of units D, B, E, A, and C and 4 spacer 1½″ × 6½″ strips, starting with a block unit and alternating with the spacer strips.

2. Sew a 1½″ × 6½″ spacer strip to the right side of a unit C.

3. Sew a 1½″ × 9½″ dark grid strip to the left side of a unit F.

4. Sew a spacer strip to the left side of a unit C.

5. Sew a 1½″ × 5½″ light fabric strip to the top of a 1½″ × 15½″ print scrap accent grid strip. Sew a 1½″ × 1½″ light fabric square to the bottom.

6. Sew 1 spacer 1½″ × 6½″ strip to the bottom of a unit F, matching the short ends; then sew another 1½″ × 6½″ strip to the bottom.

7. Sew together the 6 pieced units and 2 corner squares 6½″ × 6½″ to make a finished half-block.

8. Repeat Steps 1–7 to make a total of 2 identical half-blocks (Blocks 5 and 12).

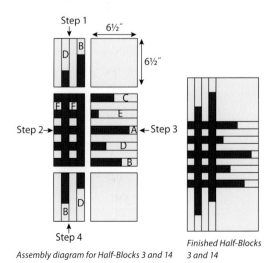

Assembly diagram for Half-Blocks 3 and 14

Finished Half-Blocks 3 and 14

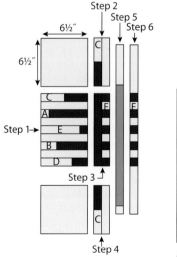
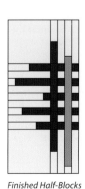

Assembly diagram for Half-Blocks 5 and 12

Finished Half-Blocks 5 and 12

Making Half-Blocks 8 and 9

Refer to the labeled parts of the assembly diagram for Half-Blocks 8 and 9 (at right).

1. Sew together 1 unit C, 1 unit E, and 2 spacer 1½″ × 6½″ strips, alternating block units and spacer strips and starting with a block unit.

2. Sew together 3 dark grid strips 1½″ × 4½″ and 3 unit G pieces, alternating the 2 and beginning with a grid strip.

3. Sew a 1½″ × 5½″ print scrap accent grid strip to a 1½″ × 5½″ light strip, matching the short (1½″) ends.

4. Sew a unit G to the left side of a 1½″ × 4½″ dark grid strip.

5. Sew together 2 spacer 1½″ × 6½″ strips, 1 unit A, and 1 unit C, alternating spacer strips and block units and starting with a spacer strip.

6. Sew together 1 each of units B, D, and A with 3 spacer 1½″ × 6½″ strips, alternating block units and spacer strips and beginning with a spacer strip.

7. Sew a 1½″ × 6½″ spacer strip to the right side of a unit C.

8. Sew together the 7 pieced units and 2 corner squares 6½″ × 6½″ to make a finished half-block.

9. Repeat Steps 1–8 to make a total of 2 identical half-blocks (Blocks 8 and 9).

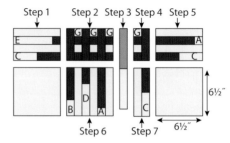

Assembly diagram for Half-Blocks 8 and 9

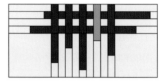

Finished Half-Blocks 8 and 9

Making the Quarter-Blocks

Blocks 1 and 16

Refer to the labeled parts of the assembly diagram for Quarter-Blocks 1 and 16 (next page).

1. Sew together 2 spacer 1½″ × 6½″ strips, 1 unit D, and 1 unit B, alternating spacer strips and block units and beginning with a spacer strip.

2. Sew together 2 dark grid strips 1½″ × 4½″ and 2 unit G pieces, alternating grid strips and block units and beginning with a grid strip.

3. Sew together 1 unit C, 1 unit E, and 2 spacer 1½″ × 6½″ strips, alternating block units and spacer strips and beginning with a block unit.

4. Sew together the 3 pieced units and a 6½″ corner square to make a finished quarter-block.

5. Repeat Steps 1–4 to make a total of 2 identical quarter-blocks (Blocks 1 and 16).

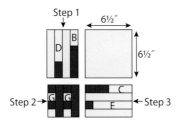

Assembly diagram for Quarter-Blocks 1 and 16

Finished Quarter-Blocks 1 and 16

Blocks 4 and 13

Refer to the labeled parts of the assembly diagram for Quarter-Blocks 4 and 13 (at right).

1. Sew a spacer 1½″ × 6½″ strip to one end of a unit G, matching the short ends.

2. Sew a 1½″ light fabric square to the top of a 1½″ × 9½″ print scrap accent grid strip.

3. Sew a 1½″ × 6½″ spacer strip to the left side of a unit C.

4. Sew a 1½″ × 4½″ dark grid strip to the left side of a unit G.

5. Sew together 1 unit D, 1 unit B, and 2 spacer 1½″ × 6½″ strips, alternating block units and spacer strips and beginning with a block unit.

6. Sew together the 5 pieced units and a 6½″ corner square to make a finished quarter-block.

7. Repeat Steps 1–6 to make a total of 2 identical quarter-blocks (Blocks 4 and 13).

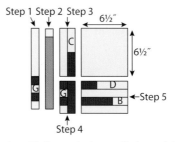

Assembly diagram for Quarter-Blocks 4 and 13

Finished Quarter-Blocks 4 and 13

Making Contrasting Block 7

The contrasting block—Block 7—is the same size and similar construction as Blocks 6, 10, and 11 (pages 111 and 112). Refer to the pieced block units (page 116).

1. Sew the 5½″ × 7″ light solid piece to the 1½″ × 7″ bright solid piece, matching the 7″ sides. Subcut this strip set into 3 pieced A units 1½″ × 6½″.

2. Sew the 4½″ × 7″ light solid piece to the 2½″ × 7″ bright solid piece, matching the 7″ sides. Cut into 4 pieced B units 1½″ × 6½″.

3. Sew the 3½″ × 7″ light solid piece to the 3½″ × 7″ bright solid piece, matching the 7″ sides. Cut into 4 pieced C units 1½″ × 6½″.

4. Sew the 2½″ × 7″ light solid piece to the 4½″ × 7″ bright solid piece, matching the 7″ sides. Cut into 4 pieced D units 1½″ × 6½″.

5. Sew the 1½″ × 7″ light solid piece to the 5½″ × 7″ bright solid piece, matching the 7″ sides. Cut into 3 pieced E units 1½″ × 6½″.

6. Sew together 5 light solid and 4 bright solid 1½″ × 7″ pieces, matching the 7″ sides. Alternate the fabrics, beginning and ending with the light fabric. Cut into 4 pieced F units 1½″ × 9½″.

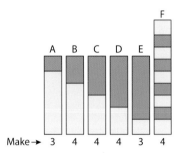

Pieced contrasting block units

7. Follow the instructions for Blocks 6, 10, and 11 (pages 111 and 112), using the bright solid fabric pieces to finish making Block 7.

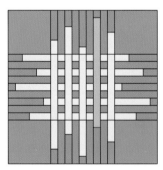

Finished Block 7

Making the Quilt Top

Refer to the quilt top assembly diagram (below) and the project photo (page 106) for the proper orientation of each block.

1. Arrange the blocks in 4 rows of 4, placing Blocks 1–4 in Row 1, Blocks 5–8 in Row 2, Blocks 9–12 in Row 3, and Blocks 13–16 in Row 4.

2. Sew together the blocks in Rows 1 and 4 with short (2½″ × 10½″) sashing strips between the blocks.

3. Sew together the blocks in Rows 2 and 3 with medium (2½″ × 21½″) sashing strips between the blocks.

4. Sew the 4 rows together with long sashing strips between the rows. Trim away any excess sashing to create a quilt top that is 68½″ × 68½″ square.

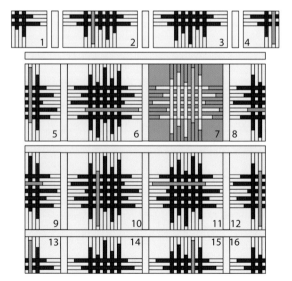

Quilt top assembly diagram

Making the Quilt Back

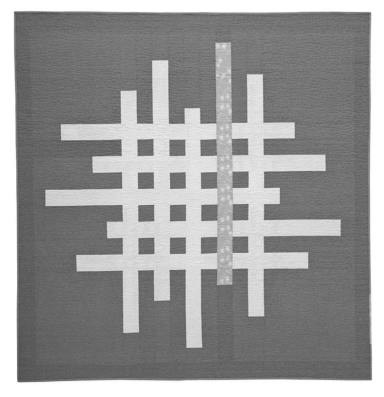

Block Units

Refer to the illustration of the pieced contrasting block units (previous page).

1. Sew the 15½″ × 15″ light solid piece to the 3½″ × 15″ bright solid piece, matching the 15″ sides. Cut into 3 pieced A units 3½″ × 18½″.

2. Sew the 12½″ × 15″ light solid piece to the 6½″ × 15″ bright solid piece, matching the 15″ sides. Cut into 4 pieced B units 3½″ × 18½″.

3. Sew the 9½″ × 15″ light solid piece to the 9½″ × 15″ bright solid piece, matching the 15″ sides. Cut into 4 pieced C units 3½″ × 18½″.

4. Sew the 6½″ × 15″ light solid piece to the 12½″ × 15″ bright solid piece, matching the 15″ sides. Cut into 4 pieced D units 3½″ × 18½″.

5. Sew the 3½″ × 15″ light solid piece to the 15½″ × 15″ bright solid piece, matching the 15″ sides. Cut into 3 pieced E units 3½″ × 18½″.

6. Sew together 5 light and 4 bright solid pieces 3½″ × 15″, matching the 15″ sides and alternating fabrics, beginning and ending with the light fabric. Cut into 4 pieced F units 3½″ × 27½″.

Quilt Back Block

Refer to the labeled parts of the quilt back block assembly diagram (page 118).

1. Sew together 1 each of units D, B, and E with 3 spacer strips 3½″ × 18½″, alternating block units and spacer strips and beginning with a block unit.

2. Sew a 3½″ × 18½″ spacer strip to the left side of a unit C.

3. Sew together 1 each of units C, E, A, D, and B with 4 spacer 3½″ × 18½″ strips, alternating block units and spacer strips and beginning and ending with a block unit.

4. Sew together 3 grid strips 3½″ × 27½″ and 3 unit F pieces, alternating grid strips and block units and beginning with a grid strip.

5. Sew together end to end the 2 print 3½″ × width of fabric accent grid strips; trim to make a strip 3½″ × 45½″. Sew the 3½″ × 3½″ bright solid piece to the top of this strip. Sew the 3½″ × 15½″ bright solid piece to the bottom.

6. Sew a 3½″ × 27½″ grid strip to the right side of a unit F.

7. Sew together 1 each of units C, A, E, B, and D and 4 spacer 3½″ × 18½″ strips, alternating spacer strips and block units and beginning and ending with a block unit.

8. Sew together 3 spacer 3½″ × 18½″ strips alternately with 1 each of units A, D, and B, beginning with a spacer strip.

9. Sew a 3½″ × 18½″ spacer strip to the right side of a unit C.

10. Refer to the quilt back block assembly diagram (below) to sew together the 9 pieced units and 4 corner squares 18½″ × 18½″ to complete the quilt back block.

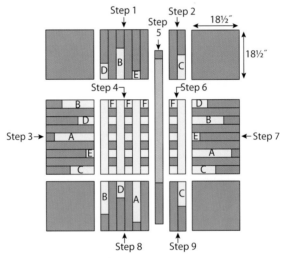

Quilt back block assembly diagram

Finishing the Quilt Back

1. Sew a 7″ × 63½″ bright fabric border strip to each side of the large block.

2. Sew 7″ × 76½″ bright fabric border strips to the top and bottom to finish the quilt back.

Finishing the Quilt

Refer to Construction Basics (pages 132–141) for details on sandwiching, quilting, and binding your project.

Alternate Ideas

make it pretty

Making the grids from a tiny floral print instead of a dark solid fabric gives this quilt a softer look, reminiscent of a garden in bloom. The key is finding a small, nondirectional print that will blend seamlessly when it is cut into small pieces. A great place to start is 1930s reproduction prints.

make it subtle

Substituting solid fabrics that are much closer in value creates a quieter mood.

Materials, Supplies, and More

Materials

Fabric

All the quilts in this book were made with mid-weight quilting cotton or cotton/linen fabric, which is durable, easy to work with, and available in a wide range of prints and colors.

Of course, quilts can be made with many types of materials, and I encourage quilters to use their own judgment and experiment with new things. Just keep in mind that the patterns in this book were designed for use with midweight cotton, and they may be more difficult to execute in another fabric.

Fabric and Design Vocabulary

The project instructions will make more sense if you familiarize yourself with the following terms that are used throughout this book.

All of the patterns use at least one **neutral solid fabric** (such as white, gray, or brown) to create **negative space**—the blank space around an object or shape. Solid sashing and other large solid areas are like the background of a quilt. Using negative space rather than filling an entire composition with prints and piecing can give your quilt a sophisticated, modern look. It may help to think of the negative space in your quilt as the wall on which you're going to hang your quilt blocks.

In most cases, the blocks in the quilt patterns will contrast with the negative space. **Contrast** occurs when adjacent fabrics are different in some way. This can be the difference in lightness and darkness (known as **value**) or the difference between brightness and dullness (known as **intensity**). It can also be the textural difference

Neutral solid fabrics

Colorful solid fabrics

between a solid and a print fabric. When a pattern calls for a **contrasting fabric,** it means a fabric that is visually different from another fabric in the composition. Some patterns also call for **coordinating fabrics,** or fabrics that match or otherwise work harmoniously together. Using a variety of coordinating fabrics can add richness and interest to a composition.

All the patterns in this book use **colorful solid fabrics** to coordinate and contrast with the print fabrics. Adding solids to the mix creates graphic, flat areas of color. For a clean, graphic look, I encourage you to select true solids rather than marbled fabrics or batiks. (The latter can be used as prints instead.)

Many of the quilts in this book create color-blocked areas by combining a variety of **monochromatic prints**—or prints that are

exclusively, or almost exclusively, a single color. Although many of the monochromatic prints in this book do include white, I avoided prints that include secondary colors (colors other than the main color in the print) and prints that are mostly white. Some monochromatic prints are so subtle that they may read as solids from a distance. These are sometimes referred to as **almost-solid fabrics.** Almost-solids can be a great addition to your quilt composition and can be used interchangeably with monochromatic prints.

Multicolor prints are exactly what they sound like: prints that include more than one color. I look for multicolor prints with regular, allover patterns that look good from multiple angles.

Monochromatic print fabrics

Monochromatic almost-solid fabrics

Multicolored print fabrics

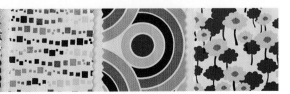

Prewashing Fabric

I usually use my fabric right off the bolt, considering this a calculated risk I'm willing to take. I've found that better-quality quilting fabrics don't run or shrink appreciably when a quilt is machine-washed using a delicate cycle, gentle detergent, and cool water.

However, I can't guarantee that you'll have the same results, and you may want to prewash fabric to rid it of any residual chemicals from the printing and dyeing process. If you decide to prewash your fabric, use the same detergent, temperature, and wash cycle you plan to use for your finished quilt. Take the fabric out of the dryer when it's still a bit damp; then press it dry.

Thread

High-quality thread will produce a much better stitch than cheap, bargain-bin alternatives. Many quilters prefer 100% cotton thread because it has the same fiber content as their fabric and batting and will, in theory, wear similarly. I also like to use 100% polyester thread (particularly for hand finishing binding and for machine appliquéing), because it's stronger and produces less lint than all-cotton thread.

Batting

Use low-loft batting to create a flat quilt that will show off your piecing and quilting work. I prefer cotton and cotton blends. Cotton battings soften in the wash, creating a pleasant crinkly texture, and should hold up to years of use.

> **tip** It may be tempting to spend a disproportionate amount of your quilting budget on beautiful fabric, but keep in mind that quality thread and batting will have a big impact on the ease of construction and the quality of your finished project.

Basic Supplies

Stock your sewing area with the following basic supplies, most of which are available at quilt shops and larger craft supply stores.

- 45mm or 60mm **rotary cutter** with an ergonomic squeeze handle

- Self-healing **cutting mat,** measuring 24″ × 36″

- 6″ × 24″ **clear plastic quilting ruler** with both grid and angled markings

- 12½″ × 12½″ **ruler** to add width to your longer ruler

- 4″ × 14″ **ruler** for working with smaller pieces

- **Iron** and **pressing board** (page 124)

- **Starch alternative,** such as Best Press

- **Sewing machine needles—** 80/12 universal for most piecing, Microtex/sharp for delicate fabric and machine appliqué, 90/14 machine quilting needle for machine quilting and piecing

- **Hand sewing needle—** size 8 embroidery sharp

- Long, sharp **quilting pins**

- Small, curved **safety pins** for pin basting your quilt sandwich

- Magnetic **pincushion**

- **Fabric scissors**

- **Utility scissors**

- **Seam ripper and snips**

- **Water-soluble marker or tailor's chalk**

- **Painter's tape**

- **Lightweight paper-backed fusible web**

- **Lightweight sew-in interfacing**

Making a Pressing Board

I prefer a pressing board to a standard ironing board. To make a pressing board, wrap a piece of plywood in three layers of batting and then cover it with muslin or other neutral solid fabric. Use a staple gun to secure the fabric and batting to the back of the plywood. Making your own pressing board lets you customize the size to fit your sewing area.

Making Templates

Translucent plastic sheets sold at quilt shops and craft stores are perfect for making reusable templates. Here's how:

1. Place a piece of translucent template plastic over your template pattern and trace the pattern onto the plastic with a permanent marker. (Or use a pencil and then wash the cut template with soap and water to remove any pencil residue.)

2. Transfer all the pattern markings onto the plastic and label the template in permanent marker.

3. Use utility scissors to cut out the template.

4. Store the templates in a large envelope with the other materials for your quilt project.

Making a Design Wall

A design wall is a sort of bulletin board for fabric—a rigid area covered with material (such as flannel or batting) that fabric will stick to. The wall can be as simple as a large piece of flannel tacked to the wall, but I prefer something a little more substantial.

My design walls were made by wrapping foam insulation with batting and using a staple gun on the back to secure the batting. Foam insulation is available at hardware stores and comes in a variety of sizes.

Homasote or Celotex fiberboard (also sold at hardware stores) can be used to make a more permanent design wall, but insulation has the advantage of being lightweight and easily portable. If you don't have a dedicated sewing room, a lightweight design wall can be tucked away in a closet or under a bed when not in use.

Keeping Things Organized

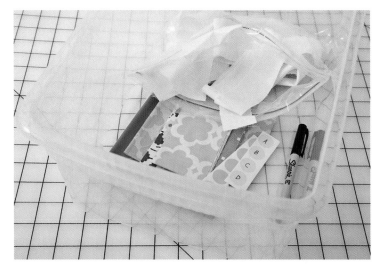

You'll probably be working on your quilt for a period of weeks or even months, so it's a good idea to have a designated space in which to keep your materials.

Store your cut pieces in a closed container to protect them from dust. I find that large, shallow plastic bins (mine are about 15″ × 22″ × 6″) are perfect for organizing a quilt project. Within the bin, store cut pieces in neat stacks (folded, if necessary), with the larger pieces on the bottom of the bin. Include any project-specific templates, notes, or supplies (such as fusible web or matching thread).

Avoid keeping the bins where they might be exposed to direct sunlight.

Scrap Basket

Fabric scraps are a wonderful by-product of quiltmaking. I encourage you to save and reuse as much fabric as you can. Many of the projects in this book include guidelines for using scrap fabric instead of new yardage for part of the quilt.

Keep a scrap bin or basket in your work area and place scraps in it as you cut. I find that I'm much more likely to use my scraps if I stack them neatly and take the time to clean them up (trimming away threads or odd shapes) before putting them in my scrap bin.

Construction Basics

Rotary Cutting Basics

note

> These cutting instructions are written for right-handed people. If you're left-handed, you'll want to do the *opposite* of what's described here. That includes moving the rotary cutter blade to the opposite side of the cutter and cutting on the opposite side of the ruler.

Rotary cutting is best done from a standing position. The vantage point gained by standing and the additional pressure you can exert on the ruler make for more accurate cutting. If possible, use your rotary cutter on a table that you can walk all the way around. This will minimize the number of times you have to move the fabric you're cutting.

> **tip** Rotary cutter blades are incredibly sharp. Always cut *away* from yourself and keep the blades covered when not in use. Avoid moving the cutter back and forth in a sawing motion, as this can chew up the fabric edges.

Make sure your fabric is free from wrinkles before you start cutting. Take the time to press the fabric before you start to work with it.

Unless otherwise noted in the project directions, always line up your ruler with the grain of the fabric. Hold the ruler firmly in place with your left hand, keeping all your fingers on top of the ruler and out of the cutter's path.

Prepare to cut by lining up the blade with the ruler's right edge. Use even pressure to run the cutter along the edge of the ruler, making a clean cut through the fabric. As you cut, be sure to keep your fingers clear of the blade.

Change your rotary cutter blade regularly. Dull or nicked blades make accurate cutting difficult and can cause ugly little pulls in the fabric. If it's taking more than one pass with the cutter to get through the fabric, it's time to change the blade.

> **tip** Save the plastic case that your rotary cutter blade came in and use it to dispose of the old blade safely or to store the blade for another use. Even after they're too dull to cut fabric, rotary cutter blades can still cut paper, template plastic, and other materials.

Cutting along the Width of the Fabric

Most of the projects in this book instruct you to start by cutting strips that are a particular size "× width of fabric." Quilting fabric is usually 40″–44″ wide; so, if the instructions call for cutting a strip 6″ × width of fabric, that means a strip of fabric that measures 6″ × about 40″–44″.

1. Place fabric, folded selvage to selvage, on the cutting mat so the folded edge is nearest you.

2. Place a 6″ × 24″ ruler on top of the fabric. Match a horizontal line on the ruler to the fold and slide the ruler to the cut edge on the right side of the fabric.

3. Square up the fabric by cutting off a tiny strip of the cut edge along the right side of the ruler, creating a straight edge that is at a right angle to the fold.

4. Move to the opposite side of the table. (If you can't move around the table, carefully turn your rotary cutting mat instead.) Now the straight edge is on the left side of the fabric, and the folded edge is away from you.

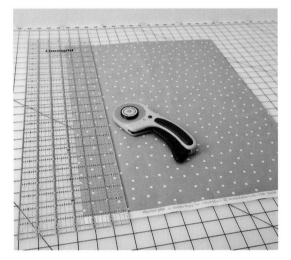

5. Use the lines on the ruler (not the lines on the cutting mat) to measure the width of the strip you want to cut, starting from the left edge; cut along the right side of the ruler. Move from left to right across the fabric as you continue making cuts.

> **tip** When cutting strips wider than 6″, use an additional ruler (a large square one works well) against the left side of your 6″ × 24″ ruler, always cutting the fabric along the right edge of the 6″ × 24″ ruler.

Cutting along the Length of the Fabric

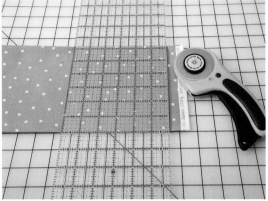

Because fabric is usually 40″–44″ wide, strips longer than this need to be cut along the length of the fabric (parallel to the selvage edge), rather than the width. To make an accurate cut, you'll need to refold the fabric to a size that fits on your mat.

Instead of folding the fabric along the existing crease, fold it in the opposite direction, bringing the cut edges together and matching the selvages along one side. Fold the fabric once or twice more, keeping the selvages along one side lined up, until you can easily place the fabric on your cutting mat.

You may need to let one end of the fabric hang off the end of the table. Just be careful not to let the weight of the fabric pull the nicely folded edge out of alignment. If necessary, hold the fabric in place with a book or another heavy object (set out of the way of your cutting tools).

Trim away the selvage to square the edge; use this edge as the straight edge for cutting the pattern pieces. You'll be cutting through more layers than when cutting along the width, so be careful to realign the edge of the fabric as needed.

Making Angled Cuts

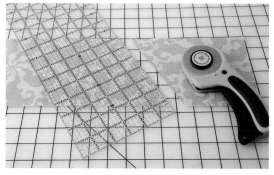

Cutting 60° angle

Most 6″ × 24″ rulers include guides for cutting 30°, 45°, and 60° angles. To use these guides, tilt the ruler to the left until the guide you want is lined up with the bottom edge of your fabric. Then cut along the right side of the ruler, just as you would if you were making a standard 90° cut.

Cutting Template Shapes

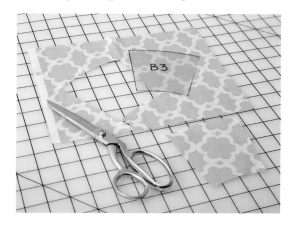

1. Place your template on the fabric, lining up any seam markers or grain-line indicators.

2. Trace around the template with tailor's chalk or a water-soluble fabric marker (avoid disappearing ink, as it may disappear before you're finished). Transfer all the necessary markings onto the fabric.

3. Cut out the template shapes from the fabric, using a rotary cutter and a ruler for straight edges and scissors for curves.

> **tip** Unless a pattern instructs you to otherwise, always trace around template shapes with the top side of the template facing up. For some shapes, tracing around an upside-down template will produce a mirror image that won't work in your quilt.

Fussy Cutting

Fussy cutting is the common term for cutting a print fabric to highlight or center a particular part of the print. One easy way to do this is to cut a piece of translucent template plastic the size of the fabric piece you need; then move it around on top of the fabric until you've framed the part you want. Cut the fabric by following the directions for cutting template shapes (at left).

Piecing Basics

Seam Allowances

The patterns in this book use a ¼˝ seam allowance. I recommend using a ¼˝ patchwork piecing foot on your sewing machine.

If you're not confident about maintaining an even seam allowance, practice with scraps before starting your actual project. Sew together two 2˝ × 2˝ squares, press the seam open, and measure the pieced unit. With an accurate ¼˝ seam allowance, the pieced unit will measure exactly 2˝ × 3½˝.

> **tip** When sewing together a pieced block and a solid piece of fabric (a piece of sashing, for instance), always keep the pieced block on top. This lets you keep an eye on the block's seam allowances to make sure they don't get pulled askew by your machine's feed dogs.

Pinning

I usually pin before sewing, inserting the pins through all the layers on both sides of each seam allowance. If there's a large space between seam allowances, I place a pin or two there as well.

Keep a pincushion next to your machine and remove the pins as you sew. All this pinning may seem tedious, but it will lead to accuracy.

When pinning together long rows of blocks or sashing, I find it easiest to line things up by placing the pieces across the end of a table. I recommend beginning in the center and working outward, instead of starting at one end. If your rows are off, doing it this way will ease in any differences across the quilt top rather than making it progressively worse as you move from one side to the other.

Pressing Seams

I press my seams open. It takes a bit more effort than pressing them to one side, as many quilters do, but I think the results are worth it. If you press the seams open, your finished blocks will be more precise, will lie flatter, and will be easier to machine quilt in an allover pattern.

Place your work right side down on the pressing surface and use your index finger to press open the seam. Run the point of your iron down the seam; then place the entire iron over the seam and press firmly. Flip the work to the other side and gently press the front (right) side.

For long seams, I usually place my work faceup on the pressing surface, press the seam to one side, and then flip the project to press the seam open.

Some quilters believe that pressing seams open will have a negative impact on the quilt's structural integrity. I have never found this to be true when using contemporary materials and machines. As long as you're using a good stitch and good materials, a quilt with pressed-open seams should be perfectly sturdy.

Machine Appliqué Basics

The type of stitch you use can affect the look of the finished appliqué. If you have a machine with lots of stitches, you may want to experiment with different stitches to find the one you like best. Machines with many stitch options may also have a special appliqué foot, which can make it easier to see what you're doing. Consult your machine manual for instructions on using the different stitches and feet.

On a simpler machine, you may only have the option of using a zigzag or a buttonhole stitch. Use the zigzag stitch for larger appliqués with finished edges, as I did for *Looptastic* (page 86), and a buttonhole stitch for raw-edge fusible appliqués, as in *Owl Eyes* (page 70).

Finished-edge appliqué on Looptastic

Getting Ready to Appliqué

1. Fit your machine with a new needle and adjust the settings for machine appliqué. Depending on the machine, this may mean using a specialty appliqué stitch, a satin stitch, a buttonhole stitch, or a plain zigzag stitch.

2. Begin on the right side of an appliqué shape. Bring the needle down in the right-hand position, just outside the appliqué; start stitching, encasing the edge of the appliqué in the

stitches. Raise the presser foot to pivot the block as necessary. *The needle should always be down before you raise the presser foot or pivot the block.*

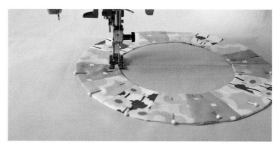

Stitching around Looptastic *appliqué*

3. When you reach your starting point, backtrack a few stitches; then remove the project from the machine and use tweezers or a seam ripper to gently pull the loose threads to the back side. Trim the threads and move on to the next appliqué.

Stitching around Owl Eyes *appliqué*

> **tip** When pivoting around convex curves and angles (such as the outside of an oval or a loop), the needle should be down in the *right-hand* position, just outside the appliqué. When stitching around concave curves and angles (such as the inside of an oval or a loop), the needle should be down in the *left-hand* position, through the appliqué piece.

Making a Quilt Sandwich

This process takes some floor space, so many of us end up doing it in a different part of our home than we normally use for sewing. Even though I have a sewing room, I find this step always involves shuffling furniture, hauling supplies into another room, and chasing away inquisitive cats. It's worth it, though, because taking the time to make a good quilt sandwich makes the next step—machine quilting—go much more smoothly.

1. Start by placing the batting on a clean, smooth floor. Spread the quilt top on the batting, smoothing out any wrinkles. (You may actually need to crawl on top of the quilt to do this.) Trim the batting to within about 2″ of the quilt top. (A)

2. Starting at the top of the quilt, carefully roll up the layered batting and quilt top. (B)

3. Continue until the batting is completely rolled up; then set the roll aside with the cut edge down. Don't worry about pinning the batting roll. The natural tendency of most battings is to cling to fabric, so the roll should hold itself together without any help from you.

4. Spread out the quilt backing fabric on the floor, right side down. Starting at the bottom of the quilt, use painter's tape to secure the edge of the quilt backing to the floor. Move to the opposite (top) edge and, pulling the quilt backing ever so slightly toward you, tape the center top of the backing to the floor. Repeat with the left and right sides and each of the corners—each time pulling very gently, but not stretching, to make sure the quilt back is completely smooth. Continue taping the edges until the backing is secure.

A *Spread the quilt top on the batting, smoothing out any wrinkles.*

B *Carefully roll up the layered batting and quilt top.*

C *Slowly unroll the batting roll onto the taped backing.*

5. Bring back the batting roll and, starting at the bottom edge, slowly unroll it onto the taped backing. You should have a few inches of leeway on all sides, but you want to make sure of two things: (1) all parts of the quilt top are inside the edges of the quilt backing and (2) the rows of blocks in the quilt top are perpendicular to the sides of the quilt backing. (C)

> **tip** This is your only chance to get the alignment of the quilt right. If you see that it's off, don't hesitate to reroll the batting and start over!

6. Once again, smooth out the quilt top and batting. I usually do this by starting at the bottom and crawling up the center of the quilt, smoothing as I go. You want to make things smooth, while also being careful not to warp the fabric as you work. If you notice that your smoothing is making the blocks wonky, ease up a bit and work them back into the right shape. (D)

7. Starting in the center of the quilt, pin curved safety pins through all the layers (top, batting, and backing). I recommend placing the pins in a grid pattern, with a pin about every 6˝. You can definitely use more pins, but keep in mind that you'll have to remove them as you quilt— an excessive number of pins may hamper your quilting progress. (E)

8. Once you've finished pinning, remove the tape and trim the quilt backing to the same size as the batting. You'll want to handle the quilt sandwich with some care. However, if you've done a good job of smoothing and pinning, you should be able to flip the sandwich over and have the back be just as smooth and even as the front.

D *Smooth out the quilt top and batting.*

E *Pin curved safety pins through all the layers.*

Machine Quilting at Home

Machine quilting at home can be an economical, personal, and fun way to finish your quilts. I quilted all the projects in this book on a home sewing machine, using either straight-line quilting with a walking foot or free-motion quilting with a darning foot.

Some General Tips

- Always start each new project with a new needle. I recommend a 90/14 universal or quilting needle.

- Use high-quality thread. Most quilters prefer 100% cotton, but today's 100% polyester threads also work well for machine quilting. Avoid poly/cotton blends or hand quilting thread, which has a waxy coating that's incompatible with machines.

- Quilting uses a lot of thread! Wind a few extra bobbins before you start.

- Stock your quilting area with a seam ripper, thread snips, and a container for collecting your basting pins as you remove them.

- Engage your machine's needle-down function (or get in the habit of using the hand wheel to manually put your needle down whenever you stop). This will hold your place when you stop, ensuring that your rows of stitching stay straight.

- The weight of your quilt hanging off the table or into your lap can work against what your sewing machine is trying to do. Make things easier by keeping the entire quilt on the tabletop while you work. Rest the quilt on your chest or even over your shoulders rather than letting it drop down into your lap.

- Machine quilting can be physically strenuous. Take breaks to relax your arms, shoulders, and neck.

- If it's been more than a year since your machine's last tune-up, it may be a good idea to have it serviced before you attempt to machine quilt.

- Machine quilting creates lots of lint. Consult your machine's manual for instructions on how to clean your machine properly. Then get in the habit of cleaning it after you finish each quilting project.

Straight-Line Quilting

The feed dogs on your sewing machine are like little teeth that cycle up and down under the fabric, pulling it through the machine. This works well when you're sewing through just one or two layers of fabric, but something as thick as a quilt needs a little more help. A walking foot (sometimes called an even-feed foot) adds a second set of feed dogs on top of the fabric. With feeds dogs on both the top and the bottom, your machine can sew through a quilt sandwich with ease.

tips for success

- Follow the manufacturer's directions to install the walking foot. Most walking feet have a bar or claw that needs to be fitted above or around the needle screw.

- Test the tension and stitch length on a practice quilt sandwich. You may find that slightly increasing both the stitch length and the tension results in a nicer-looking stitch.

- Start at or near the middle of your quilt. For instance, if you're sewing parallel lines across the quilt, start with a line through the center and work your way out to the sides, alternating the direction of each row of stitching.

- Moderate your speed. Big, clunky walking feet are fabulous tools, but they're not built to move as quickly as other feet. Using a walking foot at a very high speed can result in ugly stitches and possible damage to the foot itself.

- Avoid stitching in-the-ditch, or right on the seamline. Stitching ¼" away from the seams rather than right on top of them looks more polished—and is much easier to do!

Straight-Line Quilting Gallery

*Stitching **parallel lines** about ½" apart produces a simple quilted look and beautiful texture. Don't worry if your lines aren't perfectly straight. That's part of the charm.*

*Use a piece of blue painter's tape to randomly mark a line across your quilt. Sew along the line, reposition the tape, and repeat to create a series of **crisscrossing random lines** across the quilt top.*

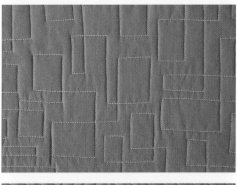

*Stopping and pivoting to make **clusters of small boxes** can be a fun way to quilt a smaller project.*

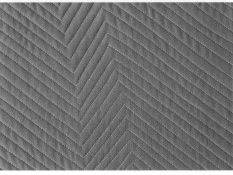

*Stitching a simple shape, such as this chevron, and then **echoing** it on both sides can produce striking results.*

Free-Motion Quilting

Most sewing-machine operations rely on the feed dogs pulling fabric through the machine to create uniform stitches. For free-motion quilting, however, you lower or otherwise disengage the feed dogs, which allows you to control the shape and size of the stitches and makes it possible for you to stitch in any direction. Lowering the feed dogs frees you to use the darning foot (sometimes called a free-motion quilting or embroidery foot) to draw circles, loops, or anything else you want on your quilt.

Getting Your Machine Ready

Consult your machine manual for information about how to prepare the machine for free-motion quilting. For most machines, you will need to fit the machine with a darning or free-motion quilting foot, set the stitch length to zero, and lower or cover the feed dogs.

Starting to Free-Motion Quilt

1. With your quilt sandwich in the machine, manually lower the needle and bring it back up again, pulling the bobbin thread through to the top of the sandwich. Put the presser foot down and make several stitches in place to create a knot.

2. Begin to move the quilt sandwich, stitching your chosen pattern for just an inch or so from where you started. Pause, making sure the

tips for success

- Free-motion quilting tends to be most successful at higher speeds. That doesn't mean you have to go as fast as you can—just fast enough to achieve smooth, fluid results.

- The key to free-motion quilting is striking a balance between the machine's speed (affected by pressure on the pedal) and the speed at which you move the quilt sandwich. If your stitches are too long, it usually means you're moving your quilt too quickly or with jerky motions. If your stitches are too small, it usually means you're not moving the quilt fast enough.

- Because you're not using the feed dogs, it's not necessary to push the quilt away from you as you

work. In fact, I find it easier to pull the quilt *toward* me, because that makes it easy to see the work that I've just done.

- Tension problems aren't always obvious from the top. Check the back of your quilt frequently to make sure everything looks right. If the bobbin thread on the back of your quilt appears to be pulled into a straight line, try increasing the thread tension.

- I find that grabbing handfuls of the quilt sandwich makes it easier for me to move the whole thing around. Other people prefer to guide the quilt with their fingertips. Experiment with different grips to find what works best for you.

needle is in the down position, and trim the loose thread ends so they won't get tangled in your work.

3. Repeat Steps 1 and 2 every time you have to rethread the machine, always making sure to bring the bobbin thread to the top and trim the loose ends.

4. Continue quilting, using your hands to guide the stitching in your desired pattern and removing safety pins as you come to them. As you practice, you'll start to get a feel for how much pressure to put on the pedal and how fast to move the quilt sandwich.

> **tip** It may help to think of your needle and thread as a pen and your quilt sandwich as paper. The twist is that with free-motion quilting, the pen stays in one place while the paper moves beneath it.

Free-Motion Quilting Gallery

This **curved, meandering stitch** creates a beautiful texture that's accentuated when the quilt is washed.

A **meandering lightning rod** pattern complements bold fabrics.

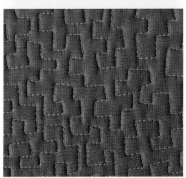

Turning curves into **boxes** lends a whimsical, retro look.

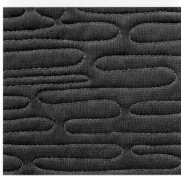

Stacked ripples contrast with regular blocky piecing.

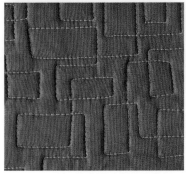

Wonky boxes with crisscrossing lines impart a modern crosshatched look.

Drawing a 2″ grid on the quilt top takes time, but it makes it easy to quilt patterns repeated in each square, such as this **dogwood flower**.

Binding Your Quilt

Binding is the finishing frame around a quilt. My favorite method is straight-grain binding made from strips cut along the grain of the fabric rather than on the bias. All the quilts in this book were made with this type of binding, which is machine sewn to the front of the quilt and finished by hand on the back.

Simple Double-Fold Binding

1. Cut binding strips along the fabric grain and trim away the selvages. Sew the strips together end to end, using ¼˝ seam allowances, and press the seams open. With the wrong sides together, press the entire binding in half lengthwise. (A)

> **tip** Straight-grain binding, or using pieces sewn together end to end, is perfect for making patchwork or scrappy binding. That can mean inserting one or two contrasting pieces between longer strips or making the entire binding from small pieces. Experiment and have fun! Just keep in mind that additional seam allowances add bulk. The extra bulk may make it difficult to achieve perfectly mitered corners, so try to keep the seams between strips away from the corners.

2. Prepare your quilt for binding by trimming all the layers even with the quilt top and squaring up the quilt top if necessary. Start in the center of one side and pin the raw (unfolded) edge of the binding to the quilt's edge. When you reach a corner, fold the binding up at a 45° angle. (B)

3. Fold the binding back toward the quilt, aligning the fold with the top edge to create a mitered corner. (C)

A *Sew the binding strips together.*

B *Trim all the layers even with the quilt top.*

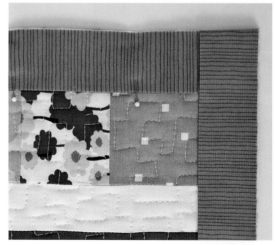

C *Align the fold with the top edge to create a mitered corner.*

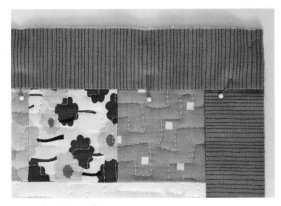

D *Pin the corner in place.*

E *Bring together the 2 ends of the binding and press in place.*

F *Sew the ends together.*

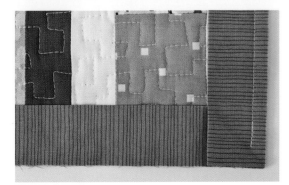

G *Sew the binding to the quilt.*

4. Fold down the mitered corner and pin it in place. (D)

5. Continue pinning, repeating Steps 2–4 at each corner, until you reach the point where you started. Bring together the 2 ends of the binding, fold each piece back onto itself so the ends are butting, and press in place. (E)

6. Match the creases you've just pressed and sew the ends together along the crease. Trim the seam allowance to ¼″, press the seam open, and pin the binding back in place. You should now have continuous binding pinned all the way around your quilt sandwich. (F)

7. Use a ¼″ seam allowance to sew the binding to the quilt. When you come to a corner, sew up to—but not beyond—the miter. Stop stitching and trim the threads. (G)

> **tip** If you'd rather not use pins, feel free to sew the binding on without pinning it first. Leave about 6″ of extra binding at your starting point. Then sew the binding to the quilt edge, folding miters at each corner, just as if you were pinning. Stop several inches from where you started and refer to Steps 5 and 6 to join the two ends of the binding.

8. Fold back the mitered corner. Resume your stitching at the corner, repeating Step 7 at each of the following corners until you reach the point where you started. (H)

9. Fold the binding to the back of the quilt—the fold you pressed into the binding earlier and the mitered corners should make this easy. Use pins or binding clips to secure a section of the binding in place.

10. To create a knotless start for hand finishing, fold a length of thread in half and thread the fold through the needle. Pull through far enough that the loose ends are near the eye of the needle and the loop is at the other end (where a knot would normally be). Pull the needle through the quilt back and batting, near the edge of the binding, leaving the end loop sticking out just a bit. Bring the needle through the edge of the binding and then back through the loop. Pull the needle until the loop closes and the thread is anchored securely. (I)

11. Hand stitch the binding in place, pushing the needle through the quilt back and batting and pulling it back up through the very edge of the binding. Continue sewing, making a stitch about every ¼˝. (J)

H *Continue sewing around the quilt.*

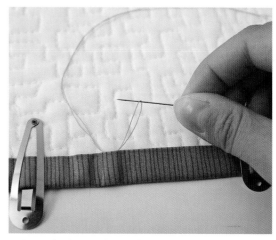

I *Create a knotless start for hand finishing.*

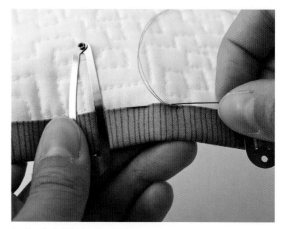

J *Hand stitch the binding in place.*

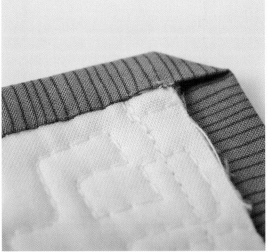

12. When you reach a corner, sew right up to the quilt's edge before folding back the mitered corner and continuing onto the next side. (K)

13. Continue until the binding is completely stitched in place. (L)

K *Sew up to the quilt's edge before folding back the mitered corner.*

> **tip** Take good care of your finished work. Quilts made with cotton generally can be machine washed and dried. I use cool water, a gentle wash cycle, and gentle detergent, and I tumble dry on low heat. If you're concerned about colors bleeding, consider trying a color catcher product. Designed to soak up any loose dye in a wash cycle, these products are usually available where laundry soap is sold.

L *Finish the binding.*

Resources

Fabrics

The Kona Cotton Solids used in this book were generously provided by:

ROBERT KAUFMAN FABRICS

robertkaufman.com

Additional fabric was provided by the following:

ART GALLERY FABRICS

artgalleryfabrics.com

CLOUD9 ORGANIC FABRIC

cloud9fabrics.com

DAISY JANIE ORGANIC FABRIC

daisyjanie.com

Most of the other fabrics I used for the quilts in this book were purchased from the following shops and online retailers:

BOLT NEIGHBORHOOD FABRIC BOUTIQUE

boltfabricboutique.com
2136 NE Alberta Street
Portland, OR 97211

COOL COTTONS

coolcottons.biz
2417 SE Hawthorne Boulevard
Portland, OR 97214

FABRICWORM

fabricworm.com

FABRIC SHACK

fabricshack.com

PINK CHALK FABRICS

pinkchalkfabrics.com

SEW, MAMA, SEW!

sewmamasew.com

Supplies

MODERN DOMESTIC

moderndomesticpdx.com
1408 NE Alberta Street
Portland, OR 97211

TABSLOT

tabslot.etsy.com
Specialty quilting templates by Jill Collins

Online Inspiration

OH, FRANSSON!

ohfransson.com
My blog

THE MODERN QUILT GUILD

themodernquiltguild.com
Find a chapter near you!

FLICKR

flickr.com
Photo sharing and many fun quilting groups

About the Author

Photo by Jen Carlton Bailly

ELIZABETH HARTMAN is a self-taught quiltmaker and designer of modern sewing and quilting patterns. Elizabeth grew up in a family whose members were always making things, and she got hooked on quilting the first time she tried it. She loves the play of color and pattern, the orderliness of the process, and—perhaps best of all—the fantastic and functional pieces that are the reward at the end. Visit Elizabeth at ohfransson.com.

Also by Elizabeth Hartman:

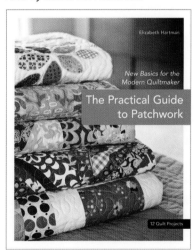

stashBOOKS®

fabric arts for a handmade lifestyle

If you're craving beautiful authenticity in a time of mass-production...Stash Books is for you. Stash Books is a line of how-to books celebrating fabric arts for a handmade lifestyle. Backed by C&T Publishing's solid reputation for quality, Stash Books will inspire you with contemporary designs, clear and simple instructions, and engaging photography.

www.stashbooks.com